TECHNICAL
REPORT

The Air Force Officer Qualifying Test

Validity, Fairness, and Bias

Chaitra M. Hardison, Carra S. Sims, Eunice C. Wong

Prepared for the United States Air Force

Approved for public release; distribution unlimited

RAND PROJECT AIR FORCE

The research described in this report was sponsored by the United States Air Force under Contract FA7014-06-C-0001. Further information may be obtained from the Strategic Planning Division, Directorate of Plans, Hq USAF.

Library of Congress Cataloging-in-Publication Data

Hardison, Chaitra M.
The Air Force Officer Qualifying Test : validity, fairness, and bias / Chaitra M. Hardison, Carra S. Sims, Eunice C. Wong.
p. cm.
Includes bibliographical references.
ISBN 978-0-8330-4779-3 (pbk. : alk. paper)
1. Air Force Officer Qualifying Test. 2. United States. Air Force—Examinations. 3. United States. Air Force—Officers—Training of. I. Sims, Carra S. II. Wong, Eunice C. III. Title.

UG793.H37 2010
358.4'1332076—dc22

2009047349

Published 2010 by the RAND Corporation
1776 Main Street, P.O. Box 2138, Santa Monica, CA 90407-2138
1200 South Hayes Street, Arlington, VA 22202-5050
4570 Fifth Avenue, Suite 600, Pittsburgh, PA 15213-2665
RAND URL: http://www.rand.org/
To order RAND documents or to obtain additional information, contact
Distribution Services: Telephone: (310) 451-7002;
Fax: (310) 451-6915; Email: order@rand.org

Preface

The Air Force Officer Qualifying Test (AFOQT) is an aptitude measure used to select officers, pilots, and combat system operators. This technical report reviews research that answers many common questions about the AFOQT, including whether the test is fair, whether it is biased against minorities or women, whether it is too expensive, whether it should be replaced, and whether it predicts the performance that is important to the Air Force. In addressing these questions, we do not produce original data analyses. Instead, we present a synthesis of the existing knowledge about the AFOQT and other selection tests and examine its implications for the future of the AFOQT.

This report was sponsored by the Air Force Directorate of Force Management Policy (AF/A1P) and conducted within the Manpower, Personnel, and Training Program of RAND Project AIR FORCE for a fiscal year 2008 study entitled "Enhanced Testing and Screening for High Value and High Attrition Programs."

This report should be of interest to anyone involved in the use of aptitude measures for hiring college graduates as entry-level personnel. This includes Air Force leadership and staff interested in the appropriateness of the AFOQT or those considering alternatives to the AFOQT, as well as other public- or private-sector organizations using similar selection measures.

RAND Project AIR FORCE

RAND Project AIR FORCE (PAF), a division of the RAND Corporation, is the U.S. Air Force's federally funded research and development center for studies and analyses. PAF provides the Air Force with independent analyses of policy alternatives affecting the development, employment, combat readiness, and support of current and future aerospace forces. Research is conducted in four programs: Force Modernization and Employment; Manpower, Personnel, and Training; Resource Management; and Strategy and Doctrine.

Additional information about PAF is available on our website:
http://www.rand.org/paf/

Contents

Figures

Tables

Summary

The Air Force has long recognized the importance of selecting the most qualified officers possible. In that spirit, the Air Force has relied on the AFOQT as one measure of those qualifications for more than 60 years.

Although the AFOQT has played a central role in the selection and placement of officers throughout the Air Force's history (see pp. 3–7), the test is not without criticism. A variety of concerns have been raised about the AFOQT, including whether the test is fair, whether the test is biased against minorities or women, whether the test is too expensive, and whether the test actually predicts anything important to the Air Force (see pp. 1–2).

To better understand these issues, AF/A1P asked RAND Project AIR FORCE to prepare a report that would review existing literature addressing common concerns about the AFOQT and would summarize the pros and cons for continuing to use the AFOQT as an Air Force officer selection tool. In doing so, we reviewed available scholarly work and relevant Air Force technical reports. Our literature search was designed to provide information addressing the following primary questions:

- What is the AFOQT?
- Is the AFOQT a valuable and useful test?
- Should the SAT replace the AFOQT?[1]
- Are there any other tests that could be used to select officers?

From that review, we conclude that the AFOQT is a good selection test. It predicts important Air Force outcomes (see pp. 14–21) and is not biased against minorities or women (see pp. 25–29). In addition, we discuss the pros and cons of replacing the AFOQT with a similar measure, such as the SAT, and conclude that the Air Force would not benefit by replacing the AFOQT with the SAT for three primary reasons. First, the Air Force cannot control the content of the SAT to ensure that the test will continue to address its selection needs. Second, certain AFOQT subtests measure specific aptitudes and knowledge needed for predicting pilot and combat systems officer success. These subtests are not covered on the SAT, and continuing to maintain them would likely negate any cost savings in switching to the SAT. Third, switching to the SAT will not help improve the racial and gender diversity of officers or pilots. Finally, we discuss the possibility of using other valid selection tools in addition to the AFOQT, such as interviews, biodata, and personality tests (see pp. 41–47).

[1] The SAT (formerly Scholastic Aptitude Test and Scholastic Assessment Test) is a standardized college entrance exam used in the United States.

Acknowledgments

Several people in the Air Force were instrumental in developing this report. In particular, we would like to thank Lisa Mills (AF/A1PF) and John Park (AF/A1PF) for their insight and guidance in the direction of the paper, Maj Gen Alfred K. Flowers and J. C. Mann for their time in explaining ROTC's use of the AFOQT, and Thomas Carretta and Johnny Weissmuller at AFPC and Paul DiTullio at the Air Force Recruiting Service for providing useful insights into common concerns about the AFOQT. We also appreciate the detailed comments regarding the legal interpretation of the Civil Rights Act provided by David Frank, Kevin Baron, and Michael Emerson. Last, but certainly not least, we would like to thank Kenneth Schwartz for his thoughts about existing issues with the AFOQT and his timely assistance in locating many of the key sources of information referenced in this document.

In addition, we would like to acknowledge three RAND researchers: Thomas Manacapilli, for his help in guiding the initial stages of this project, and Louis "Kip" Miller, for his feedback on the general outline of the manuscript, and Jeremiah Goulka, for his assistance in revising the legal discourse in the manuscript.

Abbreviations

ACT	a college entrance exam (formerly the American College Test)
AECP	Airman Education and Commissioning Program
AETC	Air Education and Training Command
AFHRL	Air Force Human Resources Laboratory
AFI	Air Force Instruction
AF/A1P	Air Force Directorate of Force Management Policy
AFOQT	Air Force Officer Qualifying Test
AFROTC	Air Force Reserve Officer Training Corps
ASVAB	Armed Services Vocational Aptitude Battery
ASCP	Airman Scholarship and Commissioning Program
DIF	differential item functioning
GPA	grade point average
GRE	Graduate Record Exam
MEPS	Military Entrance Processing Station
OTS	Officer Training School
PAF	RAND Project AIR FORCE
ROTC	Reserve Officer Training Corps
SAT	a college entrance exam (formerly the Scholastic Aptitude Test and Scholastic Assessment Test)
SDI+	Self-Descriptive Inventory
SOAR	Scholarship for Outstanding Airmen to ROTC
TDSP	Technical Degree Scholarship Program
UAS	unmanned aircraft system
USAFA	United States Air Force Academy

Glossary of Psychometric Terms

Correlation. A statistical gauge of the strength of the relationship between people's scores on two different measures (e.g., a selection measure and a measure of job performance). The correlation is the most common metric for estimating predictive validity. See p. 9.

d. A statistical measure of the standardized difference between two groups' average scores on a measure. It is calculated as the difference between the means (group 1 – group 2) divided by the average of the two groups' standard deviations. Values for *d* of 1.0 correspond to a difference of one standard deviation and are considered very large differences. Differences of 0.50 are also large, and differences of 0.30 are moderate in magnitude. See p. 22.

Disparate impact. When a facially neutral employment policy or practice has a significant adverse effect on members of a particular race, color, religion, sex, or national origin. See p. 29.

Disparate treatment. When members of a protected group (e.g., any race or gender) are not held to the same standards as any other protected group during the selection process. See p. 29.

Diversity. The proportion of minorities and women represented in the applicant pool or employee population. A reduction in the diversity of the employee population means that the employee population has a smaller proportion of minorities or women than the applicant pool. See p. 22. Note: This is the definition of diversity as it is used in this report. It is not the official Air Force definition of diversity.

Face validity. The perceived validity of a test based on how people think the test looks. This type of validity is not endorsed by professional practice as an appropriate measure of the validity of a test. See p. 35.

Four-fifths rule. When the proportion of one protected group that is hired is less than four-fifths (80 percent) of the proportion hired from the protected group with the highest selection rate (usually white or male applicants), disparate impact is presumed to exist. However, just because a test has a disparate impact does not make it unlawfully discriminatory. See p. 29.

Overprediction. When a regression line, used to predict later performance, consistently predicts performance of a protected group to be higher than it actually is. See pp. 25–27.

Predictive bias. When scores on a selection tool predict later performance differently for one group versus another (e.g., systematic over- or underprediction for a group of test takers). See p. 25.

Predictive validity. The relationship between selection test scores and important organizational outcomes (e.g., job performance, training performance, and attrition) measured later on the job. This type of validity is strongly endorsed by professional practice as an appropriate measure of the validity of a test. See p. 9.

Protected group. Any group protected by law from discrimination. For the purposes of this report, we refer to those addressed by Title VII: all races, colors, religions, and national origins, and both sexes. See p. 29.

Test validation. The process of determining whether a test is useful for predicting who will be successful on the job. See p. 9.

Underprediction. When a regression line, used to predict later performance, consistently predicts performance of a protected group to be lower than it actually is. See pp. 25–27.

Unlawful discrimination (in the context of employment). Violation of Title VII of the Civil Rights Act of 1964 (as amended), the equal protection clause of the Fourteenth Amendment of the U.S. Constitution, or other federal anti-discrimination laws. This report addresses possible violations of Title VII only. Title VII generally forbids two types of employment discrimination: disparate impact on a test that is not job related to the position in question and consistent with business necessity, and disparate treatment. Some courts have found that Title VII does not apply to military servicemembers as a matter of law. (The equal protection clause of the Fourteenth Amendment does apply to servicemembers, but it only prohibits disparate treatment.)

CHAPTER ONE

Introduction

Background

The Air Force has long recognized the importance of selecting the most qualified of the available candidates for its officer accession programs. In that spirit, the Air Force has relied on the Air Force Officer Qualifying Test (AFOQT) as one measure of those qualifications for more than 60 years.

The AFOQT is used to select college graduates for entry-level officer positions in the Air Force. It measures verbal and quantitative aptitudes for evaluating overall officer potential as well as specific aptitudes for evaluating applicant potential as a pilot or combat system operator. The verbal and quantitative aptitudes measured on the AFOQT are very similar to those on tests used to select college graduates as entry-level employees in private-sector businesses, and undergraduate and graduate students at universities across the United States.

The AFOQT is not the only aptitude test used for selection in the Air Force. The Armed Services Vocational Aptitude Battery (ASVAB), an aptitude test used to select enlisted personnel, is similar to the AFOQT in that it is designed to measure verbal and quantitative aptitude; however, it differs from the AFOQT in a number of important ways. Specifically, the ASVAB is developed and managed by the Department of Defense (DoD) and designed for use with the military enlisted population (consisting of high-school-level applicants or higher in all the military services), whereas the AFOQT is developed and managed by the Air Force and designed specifically for use with the Air Force officer population (college-level applicants and higher). As a result, the norm populations for the tests differ, the content and difficulty of the tests differ, the intended use of the tests differ, and the AFOQT includes special subtests for use in selecting people for certain officer aircrew jobs (e.g., pilots) that are not found on the ASVAB. Thus, unlike the ASVAB, the AFOQT is designed specifically for use in selecting Air Force officers.

Although the AFOQT has played a central role in the selection and placement of officers throughout the Air Force's history, it is not without its critics. As with other aptitude measures, a variety of concerns have been raised about whether the AFOQT is appropriate. Some have asked whether the test is fair, whether it is biased against minorities or women, whether it is too expensive, and whether it actually predicts anything important to the Air Force.

These questions are not unique to the AFOQT. Many organizations that use selection tests are faced with similar inquiries about their measures. For example, college admissions tests, such as the SAT, have undergone repeated public scrutiny for concerns about bias, fairness, and validity, and there has been an ongoing public and academic debate concerning the appropriateness of its use at the University of California.[1]

Some of these questions about the AFOQT are addressed in existing literature on the AFOQT and similar aptitude measures. However, for tests used in military selection, the people making policy decisions about usage and implementation are rarely the audience for whom the extant literature is written. The Air Force Directorate of Force Management Policy (AF/A1P) asked RAND Project AIR FORCE to prepare a report for the Air Force policy audience that reviews existing research and summarizes the pros and cons for continuing to retain the AFOQT as an Air Force officer selection tool.[2] This document is intended to make relevant information on this issue available to key decisionmakers in an accessible fashion. It therefore concentrates on the current selection practices in the Air Force and on consideration of alternatives to the AFOQT for selecting of Air Force officers.

Organization of the Report

Each of the next four chapters of the report addresses one of the following primary questions:

- **What is the AFOQT?** What are its applications and history?
- **Is the AFOQT a valuable and useful test?** Does it achieve the goals for which it is designed, i.e., the valid selection of personnel?
- **Should the SAT replace the AFOQT?** Would a commercially available test achieve the same goals as the AFOQT with fewer negative consequences for diversity?
- **Are there any other tests that could be used to select officers?** Could additional tests used in conjunction with the AFOQT make Air Force officer selection better?

Each chapter is organized into sections that address specific questions and concerns often expressed by test takers, test administrators, and the Air Force leadership.

We present our conclusions and recommendations in Chapter Six.

---

1 See, for example, Zwick, 2004.

2 To further this aim and enhance clarity, we have tried to minimize use of jargon and technical discussion that is typically included for an academic audience.

CHAPTER TWO

What Is the Air Force Officer Qualifying Test?

The AFOQT Today

The AFOQT is a multiple-choice test that measures a variety of aptitudes and specific knowledge areas that predict success as an officer and success in certain job training programs.

Parts of the AFOQT test are very similar to widely used aptitude and ability measures; however, others are not. For example, the AFOQT tests for verbal and quantitative aptitudes that are also included in many selection measures, such as the SAT, the ASVAB, and the Wonderlic Personnel Test. These types of aptitude tests are used by many public- and private-sector organizations because they have been repeatedly shown to predict performance across a wide variety of jobs (Hunter and Hunter, 1984; Kuncel and Hezlett, 2007a; Kuncel and Hezlett, 2007b; Schmidt and Hunter, 1998).

Less-common aptitudes and job-knowledge measures on the AFOQT are included in the test to predict performance in specific officer-level Air Force jobs. These job-specific aptitudes and job knowledge measures, such as instrument comprehension, aviation information, and table reading, distinguish the AFOQT from many of the widely used selection tests.

The current form of the AFOQT (Form S) became operational in 2005 (EASI·Consult, Schwartz, and Weissmuller, 2008) and consists of a total of eleven subtests used to form five composite scores that are computed from weighted combinations of different subtests. The subtests contributing to each composite are shown in Table 2.1.

As noted above, the various AFOQT composites are used for different selection purposes. The verbal, quantitative, and academic composites are used for officer selection; the pilot and navigator composites are used for selection into specific Air Force jobs (e.g., pilot, combat systems officer [formerly known as navigator], air battle manager, and jobs related to emerging unmanned aircraft systems [UASs]). In essence, the AFOQT serves as a tool for both general selection and job-specific selection by using the different combinations of subtests to predict success in each job.

Total testing time for the AFOQT Form S is approximately two and one-half hours. Total testing time for each subtest is also shown in Table 2.1.

Scores on the AFOQT are typically reported as percentile scores. Percentile scores range from 1 to 99 and can be interpreted as representing the proportion of applicants that generally score at or below that level. For example, a score of 55 on the verbal subtest indicates that

Table 2.1
AFOQT Form S Subtests, Composites, and Testing Times

No.	Subtests	Testing Time (minutes)	AFOQT Composites: Verbal	Quantitative	Academic	Pilot	Navigator
1	Verbal Abilities	9	x		x		x
2	Arithmetic Reasoning	30		x	x	x	x
3	Word Knowledge	6	x		x		
4	Math Knowledge	23		x	x	x	x
5	Instrument Comprehension	9				x	
6	Block Counting	5					x
7	Table Reading	9				x	x
8	Aviation Information	9				x	
9	General Science	11					x
10	Rotated Blocks[a]	15					
11	Hidden Figures[a]	10					

SOURCES: Testing time information from Lentz, Bormann, Bryant, and Dullaghan, 2008. Composite information from EASI·Consult, Schwartz, and Weissmuller, 2008.

[a] These subtests are experimental and do not currently contribute to any composite scores. See EASI·Consult, Schwartz, and Weissmuller, 2008.

about 55 percent of applicants score the same or lower on that subtest. Similarly, by subtracting the AFOQT percentile score from 100, one can determine the approximate percentage of applicants that score higher. So a score of 55 on the verbal section indicates that about 45 percent of applicant scores are higher.

The AFOQT is now administered to nearly all Air Force officer candidates and/or selectees. In 2007, more than 9,100 AFOQT tests were administered; in 2008, nearly 13,000 were administered. Testing takes place in many locations across the country including the 65 Military Entrance Processing Station (MEPS) locations, 140 Air Force Reserve Officer Training Corps (ROTC) locations, about 85 active-duty base locations, and the United States Air Force Academy (USAFA).

Who Uses the AFOQT and for What Purpose?

AFOQT scores are currently used for three main purposes: (1) selecting officers in two of the three active-duty Air Force officer-commissioning sources and in the Air Force Reserves and Air National Guard; (2) selecting officers for specialized career fields; and (3) awarding college scholarships.

The three primary commissioning sources for the active-duty Air Force are the USAFA, ROTC, and Officer Training School (OTS). Each commissioning source admits officers to the Air Force; however, the process and opportunities for admission into each commissioning source are different. The relative number of officer accessions differs by commissioning source as well. Table 2.2 summarizes the approximate number of active-duty officers commissioned through each source during fiscal year (FY) 2008.

The USAFA is a highly selective four-year college that, like other colleges and universities, relies heavily on SAT or ACT (formerly the American College Testing Program) scores to evaluate applicants. The academy reports average SAT scores of 629 and 658 for verbal and math, respectively (USAFA, 2009), which correspond to the 85th and the 88th percentile ranks on the SAT verbal and math sections, respectively (College Board, 2009a). Students applying to the USAFA are not required to take the AFOQT to be selected for the academy; however, as of 2008, all USAFA students are required to take the AFOQT to provide data for broader validity studies. Given the high selectivity of USAFA admissions and the high correlations between the SAT and the AFOQT (Ree and Carretta, 1998), students admitted to the USAFA likely would also receive high scores on the AFOQT. USAFA students are required to serve as Air Force officers after they complete their undergraduate degree.

In the Air Force ROTC, another officer commissioning source, officers are recruited and selected from students attending college around the country. Some students are offered full or partial college scholarships through ROTC. In exchange for the scholarships, those students commit to serve as Air Force officers after they complete their undergraduate degree. Students are selected to receive scholarships based on their major and their academic performance. For college students applying for an ROTC scholarship, academic potential is measured by scores on the AFOQT. Although the Air Force ROTC does not offer scholarships to all its ROTC cadets, those who do not receive scholarships can still be considered for officer commissioning through ROTC. All ROTC cadets who do not receive scholarships but are still interested in becoming commissioned officers are evaluated for commissioning, in part, by their AFOQT scores. As a result, AFOQT scores play an important role in determining who in ROTC is

Table 2.2
Active-Duty Officer Accessions by Commissioning Source, FY 2008

Source of Commission	Number Commissioned
Air Force ROTC	1,497
OTS	503
USAFA	1,016

SOURCE: AFPC, Interactive Demographic Analysis System (IDEAS) report builder, FY08 data set.

NOTE: Includes officers in each commissioning source with less than one year of commissioned service.

selected for commissioning. ROTC also commissions officers who are active-duty enlisted personnel through the Airman Scholarship and Commissioning Program (ASCP) and the Scholarship for Outstanding Airmen to ROTC (SOAR) program and considers AFOQT in their selection as well.

The third primary source of officer commissioning is OTS, which is the primary source of commissioning for applicants who have already completed a four-year college degree or higher. OTS also commissions officers who are active-duty enlisted personnel through the Airman Education and Commissioning Program (AECP) and the Technical Degree Scholarship Program (TDSP). Like ROTC, OTS selects officers based, in part, on their AFOQT scores. Therefore, all OTS applicants are required to complete the AFOQT as part of their application to OTS.

In addition to the above active-duty commissioning sources, the AFOQT is used for officer selection by the Air Force Reserve and Air National Guard.

Not only is the AFOQT used for admitting officers into the Air Force, it is also a component in selecting personnel for specific officer aircrew jobs: pilots, combat systems operators, air battle managers, and emerging UAS jobs. Actual selection criteria differ depending on the commissioning source; however, two of the three commissioning sources (ROTC and OTS) consider AFOQT scores in selecting pilots and combat systems operators and personnel for UAS jobs.

History of the AFOQT

The AFOQT was first administered in 1953 (Arth, 1986; Valentine and Creager, 1961). The first version, later named Form A, included five aptitude composites and four interest composites (Valentine and Creager, 1961) and was designed for selecting officers for advanced ROTC training.

Since then, the use of the AFOQT has expanded (Valentine and Creager, 1961) and multiple versions of the test have been developed and used for a variety of purposes. From 1954 through 1960, the AFOQT was used as a college entrance exam to select students for the USAFA. Between 1955 and 1960, the AFOQT was introduced as a test for selecting pilots and officers for officer candidate school (which became OTS in 1959), the Air Force Reserves, and the Air National Guard. Although the AFOQT continues to be used for selecting officers and pilots from multiple accession sources, its use for admission to the USAFA was short-lived; the academy replaced the AFOQT in 1960 with another college entrance exam, now known as the SAT. The use of the SAT and not the AFOQT for admissions to the USAFA continues today, but in 2008, the USAFA again began administering the AFOQT solely for the purpose of collecting data for test validation. For many years, the USAFA has administered the AFOQT to pilot applicants, but it does not use the results for pilot selection.

New test forms (after Form A) have been produced on a regular cycle, with a new form developed and introduced initially about every three years (Valentine and Creager, 1961) and now about every seven to eight years.

The development of new forms of the tests serves several purposes. First, the new forms ensure that test items remain secure. Because AFOQT scores are used to determine applicants' future career options, the AFOQT is considered a high-stakes test, and individual test takers have a vested interest in doing well. Given the high stakes, test security to prevent cheating is an important step in maintaining the utility of the test. Because items on any high-stakes test become compromised after the first administration and each subsequent time the same form is used, the possibility of cheating increases every time the same AFOQT form is used. Because the AFOQT is administered many times and at many locations every year, the best way to maintain test security is to minimize test exposure and the length of time a given test form is in the field. Thus, new items and new test forms need to be created with some regularity to protect test security.

Second, the continuous development of new items ensures that items do not become outdated. Phrases, terms, current events, and technology have changed significantly over the last 50 years; given those changes, some test questions can become antiquated or obsolete. For example, questions about aviation equipment that were current in the 1950s would not be relevant for assessing knowledge of aviation equipment today.

Third, the development of new AFOQT forms permitted refinement and improvement of the test's prediction of officer success. Technology and methods for evaluating test functioning have advanced over the years, allowing increasingly targeted improvements in the AFOQT. For example, the increased speed of data analysis made possible by today's computers now permits the quick calculation of numerous complex statistics. Because these statistical analyses can be completed in very little time, opportunities for evaluating the validity of a test have increased, as has the statistical sophistication of the validation process. In addition, as the use of standardized testing has grown, a clear set of guidelines for test validation practices has been established. The test has been revised as new analyses and established standard practices were applied, and as more test data became available. Over time, the continued analysis of the AFOQT has permitted the removal of redundant items (making the test shorter), the elimination of items that show bias against women and minorities, and the removal of items that add little to the prediction of officer success.

The AFOQT has undergone a number of structural changes as new forms were developed. Earlier versions were longer, with a larger number of subtests and a greater number of interest inventories than in more-recent versions of the test. For example, Form A included 15 subtests and Form C included 19 subtests, while the current Form S has only 11 subtests. As the test has evolved, new experimental subtests have been introduced, and some were adopted when they were determined to improve the prediction of officer success.

Another change is a shift from in-house research and development on the AFOQT to greater reliance on external contractors. Much of the earlier research and analysis of the AFOQT was published by the Air Force Human Resources Laboratory, which no longer exists. As a result, several consulting firms that specialize in the development of selection tests have been contracted to conduct the development and analysis of recent versions of the AFOQT.

CHAPTER THREE

Is the Air Force Officer Qualifying Test a Valuable and Useful Test?

When deciding whether a selection test is a valuable and useful test, we need to answer several questions:

- Is the test valid for predicting important outcomes?
- Does it affect race and gender diversity?
- Is it biased against women or minorities?
- Is it too expensive?

For the AFOQT, these questions have been addressed by past research on the AFOQT or research on similar tests. The sections that follow describe the well-established methods used by psychologists to answer these questions about employment tests and summarize existing research that may provide answers to these questions about the AFOQT.[1]

Does the AFOQT Predict Important Air Force Outcomes?

The purpose of a selection test is to improve an organization's ability to select and retain personnel who will be successful on the job. The process of determining whether a test is serving that purpose is referred to as *test validation*. There are several methods for test validation. One of the most relevant methods for validating a selection test is establishing its predictive validity.

Estimating Predictive Validity

The *predictive validity* of a selection test signifies the relationship between selection test scores and job performance. To estimate the predictive validity of a selection test, a selection test is administered to job candidates before they begin a job. After they have been on the job for a while, measures of their performance are subsequently collected. Statistical techniques are then used to assess the degree of association between selection test scores and job performance scores. The most common statistic used to estimate the predictive validity of selection tests is the *correlation*.[2]

[1] Note that the methods we describe are those that are endorsed as professional best practices in the field of personnel selection. They do not speak to the practices typically employed in the domain of employment law.

[2] Although the correlation is not the only statistic that can be used to describe the relationship between the selection test and performance, it is the most common.

Correlations can range from –1 to +1. Correlations that are positive indicate that the relationship between selection test scores and job performance are in the same direction. In other words, higher scores on the selection test are related to higher scores on job performance measures, and lower scores on a selection test are related to lower scores on job performance measures. Figures 3.1 and 3.2 are graphic representations of two positive correlations. Correlations that are negative indicate an inverse relationship between selection tests scores and job performance test scores—in other words, higher selection test scores are related to *lower* job performance scores. Figure 3.3 is a graphic representation of a negative correlation.

A correlation of zero indicates that a selection test has no relationship with job performance and therefore no predictive validity. That is, knowing a person's score on the selection measure does not provide any insight into his or her future job performance. A graphic representation of a correlation of zero is shown in Figure 3.4.

The further the validity is from zero, the better the predictive validity. Therefore, the selection test with a validity of 0.60, shown in Figure 3.1, has better (i.e., stronger) predictive validity than the test with a validity of 0.30 shown in Figure 3.2. A selection test with a predictive validity of –0.30 is equal to one with a predictive validity of 0.30. However, as shown in Figures 3.2 and 3.3, the relationships are reversed. Although predictive validities can be negative, as shown in Figure 3.3, most tests are designed such that the expected relationship with performance will be positive, as shown in Figures 3.1 and 3.2. Therefore, for simplicity, the remaining discussion about validity will refer only to positive validities in which the higher the validity, the better the test is at predicting performance.

Figure 3.1
Correlation of 0.60

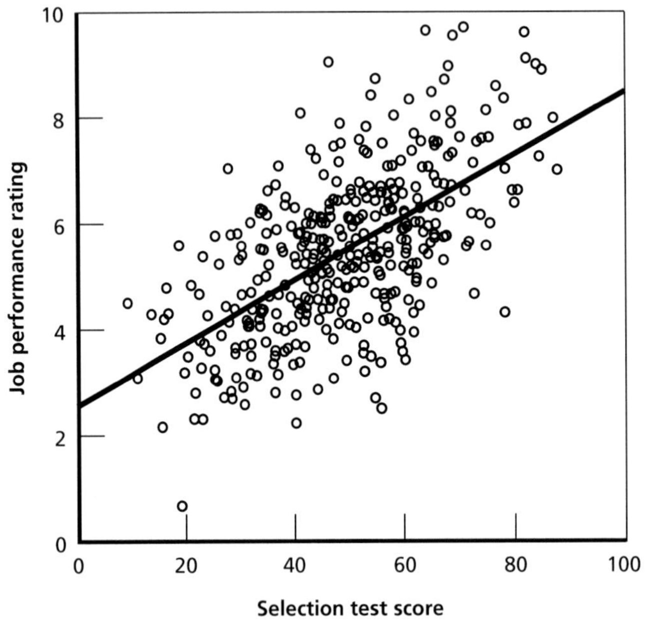

RAND *TR744-3.1*

Figure 3.2
Correlation of 0.30

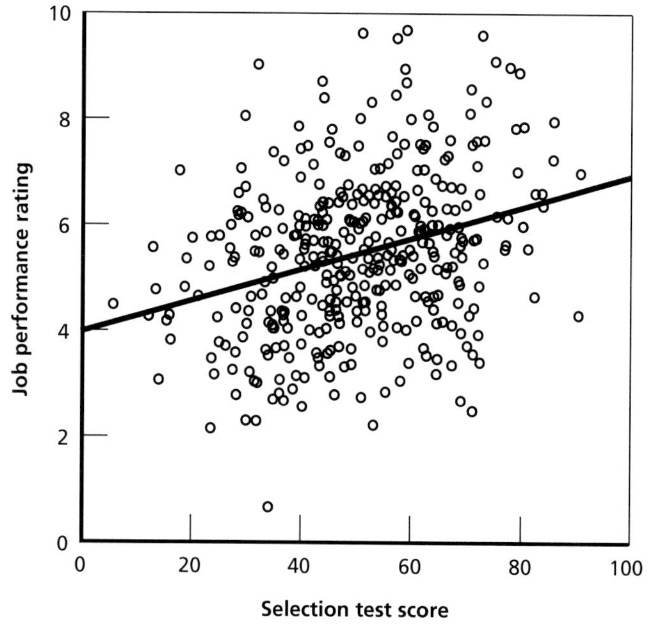

RAND *TR744-3.2*

Figure 3.3
Correlation of –0.30

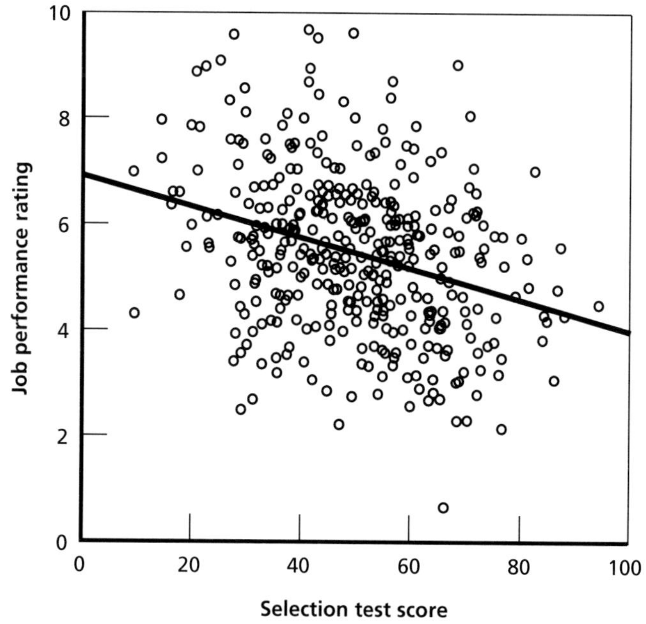

RAND *TR744-3.3*

Figure 3.4
Correlation of Zero

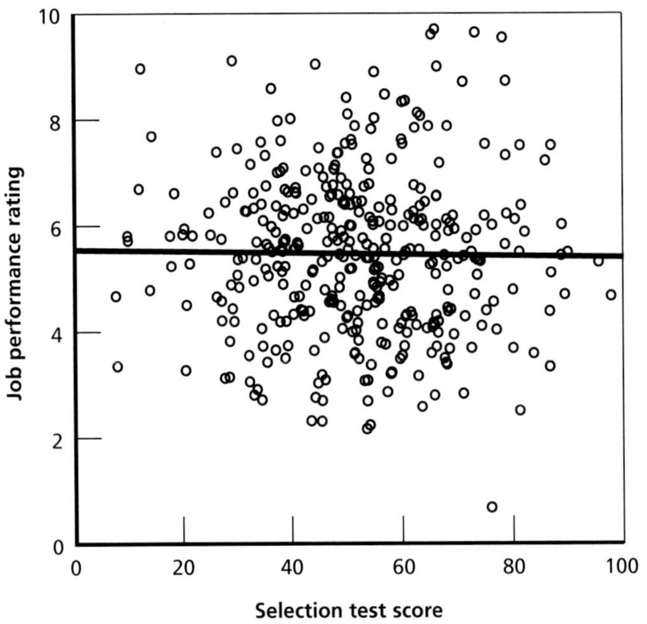

RAND *TR744-3.4*

A selection test with a predictive validity (i.e., correlation) of 1.0 indicates that the test is a perfect predictor of job performance. In other words, how well an individual performs on a selection test will *always* accurately predict how well an individual performs on the job. Selection tests with a predictive validity of 1.0 are possible in theory; in practice, however, validities are not that high. Indeed, perfect prediction is the exception rather than the rule and small correlations can still be meaningful. To illustrate this point, Meyer et al. (2001) note that the correlation between smoking and lung cancer is only 0.08, and the correlation between over-the-counter pain relievers and actual pain relief is only 0.14. In these examples, many people mistakenly assume that because the relationships are known to be valid, they are nearly perfect.

In the case of selection, there can be a similar misconception—that job performance can be accurately predicted without fail by the selection test. However, selection tests are far from perfect. Because performance on a job is determined by a number of factors that are not stable personal characteristics (such as mood, attitude, or motivation) and because observed validities can be suppressed by a number of statistical artifacts (such as whether the people selected perform better on the test on average than the broader pool of applicants), it is common for valid selection measures to have observed predictive validities that range from 0.20 to 0.40.[3] Even the best personnel selection measures seldom have validities as high as 0.50 or 0.60 (Schmidt and Hunter, 1998). Examples of other factors that can significantly affect job performance

[3] When corrections for statistical artifacts such as range restriction and unreliability in the criterion measures are applied to observed correlations, it is not uncommon to see correlations in the range of 0.35 to 0.55. For nearly all the studies of the AFOQT, corrections for range restriction or criterion unreliability were not applied.

include availability of resources (e.g., computers, funding, equipment, supplies), the quality of the environment (e.g., temperature, support by coworkers), or unforeseen events (e.g., death of a family member). Selection tests do not assess such volatile factors. Only stable individual characteristics that tend not to change over time (such as personality and aptitude) are useful for predicting people's future behavior and hence are appropriate for assessment via a selection test. A person's performance can be affected by many unpredictable events, so the reason for the typical 0.20–0.40 validity range is that the future is generally unpredictable, not that selection tests are not useful. Selection tests that achieve predictive validities of 0.30 or 0.40 are generally considered valid and beneficial for an organization unless other measures with equal or higher predictive validities are available.

Though perfect prediction should not be expected, it is worth noting that tests with less-than-perfect validities (correlations of less than 1.0) will make mistakes in prediction. Specifically, there are two kinds of mistakes in prediction: *incorrect accepts* and *incorrect rejects.* To illustrate, Figure 3.5 shows a selection test in which all individuals with scores of 60 or higher are selected for the job, and job performance ratings in which all employees with ratings of 6 or lower are considered unsuccessful on the job. If the selection test does not have a perfect

Figure 3.5
Illustration of Correct and Incorrect Decisions Using a Selection Measure

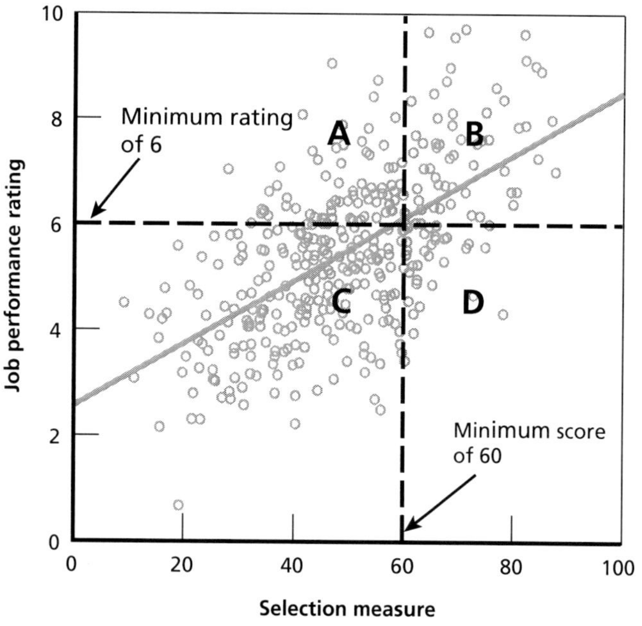

NOTE: A represents the group of people who are incorrect rejects (i.e., would not be selected, but would be successful on the job). B represents the group of people who are correct selects (i.e., would be selected and would be successful on the job). C represents the group of people who are correct rejects (i.e., would not be selected and would not be successful on the job. D represents the group of people who are incorrect selects (i.e., would be selected, but would not be successful on the job).

RAND *TR744-3.5*

validity of 1.00, there will be some individuals with test scores of 60 or higher who will *not* perform adequately. Such individuals are *incorrect accepts*, represented by the area labeled "D" in Figure 3.5. Conversely, there will be some individuals who score below the selection cutoff score of 60, but who will perform adequately. These individuals are *incorrect rejects*, represented by the area labeled "A" in Figure 3.5.

In other words, when someone receives a high score on a test with positive predictive validity, we would predict that person would do better on the job than someone who scores lower on the test. This prediction is based on the average job performance of applicants with those test scores. However, we also know that some people will perform better than predicted, and some will perform worse. Instances in which people actually perform better or worse than predicted are essentially mistakes in prediction. There will be some mistakes for any test that does not have a perfect validity of 1.00. Some people will be hired who will not do well on the job, and some people will not be hired who would have done very well on the job. However, the higher the predictive validity, the fewer mistakes will be made in who is hired and who is rejected. Because fewer mistakes in prediction are always preferred, higher validities are preferable as well. That is, the higher the validity, the more useful the test.

Several other factors can also influence the usefulness of a valid selection tool. When the ratio of the number of openings to the number of applicants becomes smaller and smaller (i.e., the organization is able to be more selective), when the number of openings to be filled becomes greater and greater (e.g., the organization is larger), and when the relative importance of making a correct selection decision becomes greater and greater (i.e., the selectees are expected to perform more and more essential tasks), the selection test is more useful (for further explanation, see Taylor and Russell, 1939).

Is There Evidence of Predictive Validity for the AFOQT?

Selection tests can be used for predicting a variety of important organizational outcomes. For the Air Force, one of the most critical and immediate outcomes for new, entry-level officers is their success in training for their career field. Several studies have examined the relationship between AFOQT scores and later officer and pilot training success, and one study has examined the AFOQT's relationship with academic performance in college.

With respect to officer training success, the most comprehensive study of AFOQT validity (Arth, 1986) examined the performance of 9,029 nonrated officers in 37 different technical training courses between 1979 and 1983.[4] According to that study, the verbal, quantitative, and academic composites of the AFOQT have statistically significant relationships with final course grades in nearly all career-field training programs. Correlations between the AFOQT composite scores and training grades were in most cases between 0.30 and 0.50 and, in a few cases, even higher. Because so many career fields were examined, this study is the clearest published evidence that the AFOQT is a valid predictor of nonrated officer training performance across a wide variety of career fields.

Additional studies lend evidence to the idea that AFOQT predictive validity generalizes to a wide variety of officer jobs. In particular, Finegold and Rogers (1985) found that the AFOQT significantly predicts a person's passing or failing the course and his or her course grades and class rank in Air Weapons Controller training. In addition, in a meta-analysis

[4] Nonrated officers are officers who are not in flying-related positions (e.g., pilots or other aircrew).

summarizing all AFOQT predictive validity evidence prior to 1988, Hartke and Short (1988) estimated that the average validity for the AFOQT academic composite was 0.39 for predicting training grades across a variety of jobs. Hartke and Short also estimated that the AFOQT validity would exceed 0.29 for more than 90 percent of Air Force specialty codes.

As noted previously, the AFOQT is used not only for selecting officers but also for aircrew selection (e.g., for pilots, combat systems operators, and other aircrew), and predictive validity evidence is available here as well. For example, Carretta (1987) found that AFOQT scores weakly but statistically significantly predict whether students pass or fail undergraduate pilot training and Advanced Training Recommendation Board ratings (validities of 0.11 and 0.14, respectively). However, using a larger sample of undergraduate pilot trainees, Carretta and Siem (1988) reported a much stronger relationship for the AFOQT with both undergraduate pilot training outcomes and Advanced Training Recommendation Board ratings—0.29 and 0.27, respectively.

Another study (Ree, Carretta, and Teachout, 1995) examined the relationship between training scores and the AFOQT for 3,428 pilot trainees. Their results show a strong direct relationship between AFOQT scores (as measured by the verbal and quantitative composites) and job knowledge acquired during pilot training. They also found that job knowledge acquired in training is strongly related to actual flying scores during pilot training. Based on those findings, they concluded that using AFOQT verbal and quantitative composites to select personnel for pilot training should lead to improved training performance and ultimately better performance as pilots on the job.

More recently, Carretta (2005) reconfirmed that AFOQT scores predict pilot success. He found that the AFOQT predicts whether students in specialized undergraduate pilot training pass or fail the T-37 training, as well as students' final T-37 training grades.[5] While Carretta found that all AFOQT composites were significantly related to both pilot training outcomes, the relationships were the strongest for the pilot composite—0.31 and 0.34 for T-37 pass/fail and final grades, respectively.

In addition to evidence that the AFOQT predicts success in pilot training and officer training programs, one study has shown that the AFOQT is a good predictor of college grades. Diehl (1986) examined the relationship between the AFOQT academic composite scores (i.e., combined verbal and math composites) and college grade point average (GPA) for 3,573 ROTC cadets and found that the academic composite had a correlation of 0.21 with GPA.

In sum, the studies described above have shown repeatedly that the AFOQT is a valid predictor of important Air Force outcomes across a variety of jobs. As noted previously, correlations of 0.30 or 0.40 between predictors and outcome variables (such as training success) are generally considered acceptable evidence that a selection test is a valid predictor of the outcome. This level of validity and higher has been demonstrated repeatedly and consistently for the AFOQT to predict an array of outcomes for a variety of jobs.[6] This supports the contention that the AFOQT (or another test that measures similar constructs) should be used to select officers.

---

[5] The T-37 is a type of airplane used in the Air Force during pilot training.

[6] With the exception of Carretta, 2005, who applied corrections for range restriction, no corrections for range restriction or unreliability in the criterion were applied to the estimates of AFOQT validity; hence, the validities reported in this section are conservative and likely underestimate the true relationships.

Can Validity Change?

Sometimes, people who are not familiar with test validation wonder whether a test should be validated every year. Essentially, they think that just because the test was validated two years ago (or more, as in the case of some of the studies of AFOQT validity), this validation evidence is dated and not applicable to the present. In actuality, the validity of a test like the AFOQT, which measures verbal and quantitative aptitudes to predict job performance, is not likely to change from year to year.

Many researchers have examined numerous studies of aptitude measures across a variety of contexts and jobs, and those researchers agree: Measures of general aptitude do predict job performance (e.g., Hunter and Hunter, 1984). More than 85 years of research, including thousands of studies on aptitude measures, confirm that general aptitude (or cognitive ability) is the best predictor of training success, the best predictor of job knowledge acquisition, and the best predictor of job performance for people with no prior work experience (Schmidt and Hunter, 1998). This finding generalizes across jobs: Validities for predicting performance increase as the level of complexity of the job increases, with the highest validities associated with predicting performance in professional managerial jobs (Hunter and Hunter, 1984). Based on thousands of studies of tests similar to the AFOQT and the work of numerous researchers who have reviewed those results, there is a consensus that if a test measures general mental aptitudes (or abilities), that test will be a good predictor of later performance. And the AFOQT measures these same general aptitudes and abilities.

Nevertheless, that does not negate the need to periodically validate and update a test like the AFOQT. While the validity of general aptitudes is unlikely to drastically differ across job types or from year to year, the validity of a test that is intended to measure aptitudes may decline eventually for at least two reasons.

First, test items can become outdated. For example, the meanings of some of the individual items may change as language itself changes or as exposure to a topic area changes from decade to decade (Chan, Drasgow, and Sawin, 1999).[7] As noted previously, this is one reason that new forms of the AFOQT are developed every several years. The development of new test items is a hallmark of quality assessment rather than an indication of a problem with a particular form of the test.

Although some test items can become outdated in a matter of years or even months, certain types of test items do not become dated as quickly. For example, items focused on basic skills and principles, such as tests of arithmetic reasoning and paragraph comprehension, tend to be more resistant to change than more semantically laden areas, such as tests of electronics information (Chan, Drasgow, and Sawin, 1999). Because much of the AFOQT includes items focused on basic skills and principles, the development of new test items every several years is sufficient to keep the test current.

Second, the size of a validity estimate may decrease as the time between the aptitude test scores and the measure of performance increases (Hulin, Henry, and Noon, 1990; Keil and Cortina, 2001), although this does not always occur. To illustrate an instance in which it might occur, if test scores are collected before training and training occurs before the person begins working on the job, then the test scores would be expected to predict training performance better than job performance. This does not negate the value of aptitude testing for predict-

---

[7] For example, test takers in 2008 may find items addressing weather patterns easier to answer than did test takers in past decades because recent media coverage of climate change has increased exposure to such issues.

ing job performance. Over time, people learn, gain experience, and choose to take advantage of opportunities (or not) that affect their job performance. In our example of employees who are tested prior to training, trained, and then given the chance to perform on the job, we would expect that the training itself would predict job performance. Because of these other influences, the impact of aptitude on job performance over time can weaken as time passes. Although longitudinal studies that track employees from the point of selection through later job performance (and hence account for developmental effects) are relatively sparse, Keil and Cortina (2001) summarized the research that does exist and found that general aptitude measured by instruments similar to the AFOQT is predictive of performance for approximately three and one-half years. Although their data were cross-sectional rather than longitudinal, Schmidt et al. (1988) present data suggesting that performance differences between high-aptitude and low-aptitude workers persist up to five years on the job. Other research summarized by Gottfredson (1997) suggests that aptitude is, in essence, the ability to deal with complexity; that it is essential for success in complex environments; and that the impact of aptitude is cumulative. Gottfredson indicated that as experience accrues, the *direct* effects of aptitude are potentially less evident but nonetheless persist via their relationships with trainability and the speed of learning new skills. Moreover, if job complexity itself increases, aptitude may even be more essential to job performance over time.

However, there is no published validity evidence confirming that the AFOQT predicts long-term officer performance. All the studies discussed in the previous section have validated the AFOQT for predicting training performance or academic performance and critical entry-level officer and ROTC recruit outcomes. However, Air Force outcomes of more long-term importance, such as retention and promotion, could be investigated as well.

Is the AFOQT Being Used Optimally in the Selection System?

Although we have presented evidence showing that the AFOQT has good predictive validity, this does not mean that the Air Force officer and aircrew selection process (i.e., the overall selection system) also has good predictive validity. More specifically, the validity of the AFOQT only provides insight into the validity of the Air Force's selection system under two specific conditions. The first condition is that the full AFOQT score range is utilized rather than a minimum cut score (i.e., pass/fail), and that the people with the highest scores are selected first. This manner of selection is referred to as "top-down selection." The second condition is that the AFOQT is not being combined with measures that fail to add to prediction. If either of these conditions is not met, the AFOQT is not being used optimally in the officer selection system. In fact, neither of these conditions appears to be consistent with how the AFOQT is used in the Air Force selection system.

The Full Range of AFOQT Scores Is Not Utilized

The Air Force does not use the full range of AFOQT scores. Instead, it has established minimum cut scores for each composite. Table 3.1 summarizes the Air Force's minimum AFOQT requirements for various occupations and commissioning sources.

Table 3.1
Minimum Percentile Scores on the AFOQT for Qualifying as an Officer, Pilot, and Combat Systems Operator

	Minimum AFOQT Composite Percentile Score				
Occupation	**Pilot**	**Navigator**	**Pilot + Navigator**	**Verbal**	**Quantitative**
Officer (OTS and ROTC)	NA	NA	NA	≥15	≥10
Combat systems operator (OTS and ROTC)	≥10	≥25	≥50	≥15	≥10
Pilot (ROTC)	≥25	≥10	≥50	≥15	≥10
Pilot (OTS), private pilot's license	≥25	≥10	≥50	≥15	≥10
Pilot (OTS), no private pilot's license	≥50	≥10	≥60	≥15	≥10

SOURCES: For officers, combat systems operators, and ROTC pilots, AFI 36-2013, 2006. For OTS pilots, AETC Instruction 36-2002, 1999.

NOTE: Percentile scores range from 1 to 99.

As shown in Table 3.1, none of the commissioning sources is required to use top-down selection.[8] Instead, there is a minimum cut point below which candidates are considered not qualified and above which any candidate may be selected.

Use of a minimum qualification score can reduce the validity of the selection system when some personnel with lower AFOQT scores are selected instead of more-qualified applicants with higher scores on the AFOQT. In general, the lower the minimum cut score is relative to the average score of the applicant pool, the more validity the selection system can lose.[9]

In addition, if the AFOQT is used differently across commissioning sources, AFOQT validity will also differ across commissioning sources in practice. With respect to the minimum cut point for selecting pilots, there are already noticeable differences between OTS and ROTC because OTS has a higher requirement for pilots than ROTC when the applicant does not already possess a private pilot's license.

Less-Valid Measures Can Hamper the Validity of the Selection System

The second reason the AFOQT test may not be used optimally is that other, possibly less-valid, measures are used to select among those applicants who meet the minimum AFOQT qualification score. Using other selection measures in addition to the AFOQT could improve the validity of an overall selection system, but only if those other measures are highly valid predictors of important Air Force outcomes that are not highly correlated with the AFOQT. But if the other selection measures are low-validity predictors and their influence on the selection system is weighted greater than zero (i.e., they have some influence on the decision rather than being ignored), they will *decrease* the validity of the overall selection system. If the other selection measures are highly valid but also highly correlated with the AFOQT, then they will not increase the validity of the selection system.

[8] Although top-down selection is not required, it is possible that the various commissioning sources might, at times, decide to employ top-down selection with the AFOQT.

[9] For an examination of the effect of dichotomizing test scores on correlations, see Cohen, 1983.

Although the OTS and ROTC selection systems are not completely transparent, they do use other measures besides the AFOQT. Some of those measures include interviews, evaluations of moral character and leadership potential, college or high school GPA, physical ability tests, and recommendations (Ingerick, 2006). However, Ingerick indicates that ROTC and OTS use a number of tools without "substantive and clear specifications of what they intend to measure" (p. 33), which presents a potential threat to the validity of the selection systems.

We are not aware of any research on the validity of the other selection measures for predicting Air Force outcomes, but it is likely that these measures do not have predictive validities as high as the AFOQT. If the other selection measures have lower validities but contribute more to selection decisions than the AFOQT, then the resulting selection decisions (i.e., the whole selection system) would have a lower validity than decisions based solely on the AFOQT.

ROTC and OTS do weight the other, possibly less-valid, selection tools much more heavily than the AFOQT in their selection systems. For example, ROTC weights the "Relative Standing Score" far more heavily in their selection system than the AFOQT score (50 percent versus 15 percent; Ingerick, 2006). Ingerick indicates that it is not clear what the Relative Standing Score contains (although it appears that an interview assessing seven dimensions, including character and core values, self-confidence, and human relations, may be incorporated into this score). If 85 percent of the selection system is based on measures that are less valid than the AFOQT, then the selection system is less valid than using the AFOQT in isolation.

In contrast to ROTC, it is impossible to tell exactly how much weight is given to either the interview or the AFOQT in the OTS selection system. Interview information is somehow combined with letters of recommendation, communication skills, and legal violations into an evaluation of an applicant's "Potential/Adaptability" (Ingerick, 2006) and AFOQT scores are somehow combined with academic major, GPA, and college transcripts for an evaluation of "Education/Aptitude" (Ingerick, 2006). In the OTS selection system, Potential/Adaptability and Education/Aptitude are then each given a 33 percent weight. In essence, it appears that the AFOQT's contribution to the overall selection systems in ROTC and OTS is small relative to other selection measures for both commissioning sources.

Differing Commissioning Source Quotas Can Inhibit the Validity of the Selection System

The AFOQT should be the centerpiece of the selection system because of its high validity. However, the quotas provided for selection within each commissioning source inhibit the validity of the selection system by bounding the effectiveness of the AFOQT. If the Air Force specifies that an arbitrary percentage of new officers should come from ROTC without considering the qualifications of the available pool of ROTC applicants, it disregards the possibility that ROTC may be forced to select applicants that are of lower quality than are available through other commissioning sources. Similarly, other commissioning sources may deny jobs to highly qualified applicants because their quota is full. In fact, it appears that the ROTC applicant pool is different from the OTS applicant pool. For example, Table 3.2 summarizes data reported in the EASI·Consult, Schwartz, and Weissmuller (2008) study of subgroup qualification rates, which shows that OTS has a larger proportion of black and Hispanic applicants for officer positions who meet the minimum qualifications than does ROTC. Results are simi-

Table 3.2
Percentage of OTS and ROTC Applicants Meeting the Minimum AFOQT Qualifications for Each Job Category by Race/Ethnicity

		White	Asian	Black	Hispanic
Source	Meeting Qualifications Set for:	Percent passing			
OTS	Pilot with private pilot's license[a]	85	65	35	60
OTS	Pilot without private pilot's license[a]	63	46	15	39
OTS	Combat systems operator	85	66	38	59
OTS	Officer	93	78	66	78
ROTC	Pilot	81	62	31	54
ROTC	Combat systems operator	81	66	36	54
ROTC	Officer	88	73	59	68

SOURCE EASI·Consult, Schwartz, and Weissmuller, 2008.

[a] This table compares AFOQT scores for all OTS applicants with the minimum AFOQT score requirements for each pilot standard, regardless of their actual pilot license status.

NOTE: OTS applicant sample sizes: white n = 3,657, Asian n = 242, black n = 602, and Hispanic n = 477. ROTC applicant sample sizes: white n= 8,368, Asian n = 572, black n = 1,148, and Hispanic n = 1,122.

lar, though less pronounced, for white and Asian applicants. In general, this suggests that the AFOQT scores of OTS applicants are slightly higher than those of ROTC applicants.[10]

To implement top-down selection, the Air Force should select the candidates with the highest scores on the AFOQT, regardless of commissioning source. Given the applicant pool differences, using a quota to restrict the number of high-AFOQT applicants from OTS in favor of lower-AFOQT applicants from ROTC puts an artificial upper bound on the effectiveness to be had by employing the AFOQT with top-down selection.

Because OTS is customarily used to fill in areas of officer expertise that are not sufficiently filled via the USAFA and ROTC, its quotas are a direct outcome of what is and is not available in the USAFA and ROTC pools. Therefore, it is not possible for the OTS and ROTC selection systems to be used simultaneously in top-down selection. An alternative possibility would be to reduce the contribution of ROTC and expand the contribution of OTS. This would both accommodate a potentially greater number of high-quality applicants and fill in needed areas of expertise.[11]

---

[10] There are multiple explanations for why average AFOQT scores are higher in OTS than in ROTC. The number of years of college may influence AFOQT scores. If that is true, then, compared with ROTC candidates who take the AFOQT as early as their freshman year, OTS applicants who have completed at least four years of college would appear to score better—even if there are no real aptitude differences. Additionally, OTS takes applicants with graduate degrees (e.g., lawyers, medical doctors), while ROTC does not. Scores of applicants with graduate degrees might pull the OTS average up even if those with four-year degrees score no differently. Last, OTS might simply attract higher-aptitude candidates than ROTC does.

[11] Based on the characteristics of the OTS and ROTC applicant pools and other organizational constraints, linear programming models could be used to adjust the flow of selectees through OTS and ROTC to achieve an optimal mix of OTS and ROTC selectees for maximizing the mean AFOQT scores of incoming officers. For an example application of linear programming to Air Force personnel issues, see Robbert et al., 2004.

One argument against reducing the ROTC quota is that the ROTC commissioning path is longer and allows for greater exposure to Air Force culture. Nevertheless, the trade-off of acculturation for quality is not advantageous. Acculturation can be accomplished after commissioning, while improvement in quality cannot. In addition, given that the percentage of minority applicants who meet the minimum cut point is higher for OTS than for ROTC, the current quota system may even be limiting another Air Force goal: the diversity of officer selectees.

Other Selection Measures Could Improve the Validity of the Selection System

As noted previously, it is possible for the use of other measures to improve a selection system. However, that would require that the measures be both highly valid and not highly correlated with the AFOQT. For example, this could be accomplished with an interview, and, in fact, both ROTC and OTS use candidate interviews (Ingerick, 2006). Ingerick indicates that ROTC interviews are designed to assess the dimensions of character and core values, self-confidence, human relations, planning and organizing, communication skills, leadership, and motivation toward the Air Force. These dimensions do not seem strongly related to aptitude, but it is impossible to tell without more information. While it is not completely clear whether OTS and ROTC use the same interview structure and format, Huffcutt, Roth, and McDaniel (1996) indicate that the average relationship between interviews and aptitude tests is fairly high (0.40), which suggests that substantial overlap between Air Force interviews and AFOQT scores is a definite risk.[12] To the extent that any assessment tool (such as an interview) is measuring content similar to that of the AFOQT, utilizing that tool in addition to the AFOQT will not add to the predictive power of the selection system because it provides relatively little additional important predictive content. It is even possible that using additional measures may in fact be causing far more harm than good by effectively replacing a valid and reliable test with a less-valid, less-reliable measure of the same content material.

Other Selection Measures Should Be Validated

In sum, it appears that the AFOQT is not used optimally in current practice. The validity estimates for the AFOQT represent the validity that could be obtained, not the validity that is actually obtained in the current selection systems. If the Air Force wants the most valid process for selecting officers, additional sources of information that are currently considered in officer selection—interviews, judgments of moral character and leadership potential, college or high school GPA, physical ability tests, recommendations, etc., and their relative weights—also need to be validated. Doing so would entail examining the overlap between these other sources of information and AFOQT scores to determine the most valid method of combining the various pieces of information about applicants. Once the most valid method of combining information is known, that method should be applied consistently and equivalently across all commissioning sources.

---

[12] Interviews may be developed specifically to mitigate this risk. For example, Huffcutt, Roth, and McDaniel (1996) found that the relationship between aptitude tests and interviews was weaker when the interviews were more structured. A structured interview has a number of characteristics, the most prototypical being that the same questions are used for all applicants rather than the interviewer having complete freedom to determine the content of the interview (e.g., Campion, Palmer, and Campion, 1997; Dipboye and Gaugler, 1993). Huffcutt, Roth, and McDaniel also indicated that the type of structure might be important (e.g., behavior description interviews had very low overlap with aptitude).

Does the AFOQT Affect Race and Gender Diversity?

Many organizations value diversity, and the Air Force is certainly no exception. However, if applicants from some groups (i.e., races or genders) tend, on average, to perform better on a selection test than other groups, the use of that selection test will result in a workforce that is not identical to the race and gender makeup of the applicant pool. The larger the average differences in selection test scores across races or groups, the greater the differences in diversity between the applicants and those selected. In other words, group differences on selection test scores can reduce diversity.[13]

Are There Group Differences in AFOQT Scores?

In short, yes. Like tests in many other organizations, tests used by the Air Force to screen officer candidates and select personnel for pilot training and other aircrew jobs do, on average, show differences in scores across races and genders. Use of these measures to select personnel can therefore result in a reduction in the race and gender diversity among officers as well as pilots and other aircrew personnel.[14]

Data from EASI·Consult, Schwartz, and Weissmuller (2008) illustrating the magnitude of the group differences on AFOQT scores are presented below in Tables 3.3 and 3.4. Table 3.3 shows the average percentile scores for men and women on each of the composite scores. The column labeled *d* shows the difference in standard deviation units, which is one measure

Table 3.3
AFOQT Composite Scores by Gender

	Male (n = 15,574)		Female (n = 4,971)		
Composite Percentile Score	Mean	Standard Deviation	Mean	Standard Deviation	*d*
Verbal	54.05	28.14	45.26	28.85	–0.31
Quantitative	58.61	27.53	45.21	27.63	–0.49
Academic	57.36	27.77	44.44	28.42	–0.46
Pilot	60.82	26.16	36.03	24.52	–0.98
Navigator	58.78	27.06	43.56	27.66	–0.56

SOURCE: Applicant statistics on AFOQT Form S from EASI·Consult, Schwartz, and Weissmuller, 2008.

NOTE: *d* is the standardized difference between the female mean and the male mean. It is calculated as the difference between the means (female – male) divided by the average of the two standard deviations.

[13] Autor and Scarborough (2008) point out that this is true only to the extent that a selection test score provides new information that is unfavorable to minority applicants. Some of the same information regarding performance potential may be acquired through an existing selection process; hence, the institution of a selection test may not actually make a difference in the diversity makeup of the organization.

[14] Note that diversity can be defined in a number of ways. When we refer to diversity in this report, we mean the proportion of minorities and women represented in the applicant pool or employee population. When we refer to a reduction in the diversity of the employee population, we mean that the employee population has a smaller proportion of minorities than the applicant pool.

of the magnitude of the difference. Values for *d* of 1.00 correspond to a difference of one standard deviation and are considered very large differences. Differences of 0.50 are also large, and differences of 0.30 are moderate in magnitude (Cohen, 1992).

The differences between the average scores of men and women range from moderate to very large depending on the composite. For example, for the quantitative composite, the average score for women is about a half a standard deviation (0.49) lower than the average score for men. The difference for the verbal composite is smaller, with women 0.31 standard deviations lower than men. The largest difference is for the pilot composite, with nearly one standard deviation difference between the genders.

Table 3.4 shows the average scores by race and the standardized differences between each racial group's mean and the white mean. This table shows that the difference between the black mean and the white mean (ranging from –0.88 to –1.52) is very large for all composite scores. The differences between the Hispanic and white means are smaller but still large (ranging from –0.57 to –0.71). For the Asian and white means, the differences range from no meaningful difference on the quantitative composite to moderate and large on the other composites.

Considering the average percentile scores is another way to interpret the differences. The average score for women on the quantitative section of the AFOQT is at the 45th percentile, while the average score for men is at the 54th percentile.

The average percentile scores are lowest for black applicants—by a noticeable margin. The black verbal and quantitative averages are at the 34th and 33rd percentiles respectively. A comparison with the white averages (57th and 60th percentiles, respectively) shows clearly that the use of the AFOQT for selection of officers will result in less diversity in the officer pool than there is in the applicant pool.

Other studies of the AFOQT also have found similar significant group differences in AFOQT composite mean scores across gender and minority group status. A study conducted with 13,559 Air Force officer cadets who entered OTS between 1982 and 1988 showed that black cadets scored 0.50 standard deviations lower than white cadets (i.e., $d = -0.50$) on the

Table 3.4
AFOQT Composite Scores by Race/Ethnicity

	White (N = 14,773)		Black (N = 2,039)			Hispanic (N = 1,908)			Asian (N = 954)		
Subtest	**Mean**	**SD**	**Mean**	**SD**	*d*	**Mean**	**SD**	*d*	**Mean**	**SD**	*d*
Verbal	56.93	27.37	33.65	25.27	–0.88	39.77	27.61	–0.62	43.07	29.02	–0.49
Quantitative	59.86	26.70	33.05	24.60	–1.05	44.44	27.48	–0.57	59.07	29.15	–0.03
Academic	59.67	26.78	30.91	24.32	–1.13	40.99	27.68	–0.69	51.56	28.67	–0.29
Pilot	61.31	25.44	25.42	21.80	–1.52	42.71	26.72	–0.71	48.81	26.85	–0.48
Navigator	60.74	25.85	28.46	23.28	–1.31	42.45	27.43	–0.69	54.88	28.34	–0.22

SOURCE: Applicant statistics on AFOQT Form S from EASI·Consult, Schwartz, and Weissmuller, 2008.

NOTE: *d* is the standardized difference between the mean for the corresponding group and the mean for white applicants. It is calculated as the difference between the means divided by the average of the two standard deviations.

AFOQT verbal, quantitative, and academic ability test composites (Roberts and Skinner, 1996). Interestingly, this study revealed more-varied gender differences in AFOQT composite scores. Specifically, female cadets scored on average 0.33 standard deviations higher than male cadets on the verbal composite, but 0.33 standard deviations lower on the quantitative composite. No significant gender differences were found on the academic ability composite mean scores.

Carretta (1997) examined scores on the AFOQT for 269,968 Air Force applicants and 9,476 Air Force pilot trainees. Group differences were examined across AFOQT composites and individual subtests. Among Air Force applicants, black and Hispanic applicants obtained significantly lower scores than white applicants on all five composites (verbal, quantitative, academic ability, pilot, and navigator-technical) and all 16 subtests. Similarly, female applicants scored significantly lower than males on all the composite tests and on 15 of the 16 subtests. Among the sample of Air Force officer pilot trainees, comparable ethnic group differences were found as well. Black and Hispanic trainees obtained lower scores on all the composites and most of the subtests than did white trainees. However, fewer gender differences were found. Compared with male trainees, females obtained lower mean scores solely on the navigator-technical composite and the aircrew and spatial subtests. Prior studies have also found lower performance on AFOQT pilot and navigator-technical composites by female pilot trainees compared with male pilot trainees (Carretta, 1990).

This finding of group differences is not unique to the AFOQT, nor is it inconsistent with those observed on similar selection measures. Roth et al. (2001) examined all existing studies of aptitude measures and reported the average differences between black and white test scores across those studies. For example, they report an average standardized black-white differences of $d = -0.98$ for college applicants taking the SAT or ACT college entrance exams, $d = -1.19$ for military applicants taking the ASVAB, and $d = -1.34$ on the Graduate Record Exam (GRE). They also report average standardized Hispanic-white differences on the same tests ranging from –0.53 to –0.85. These differences are not unlike those reported for the AFOQT. Group differences for the SAT are discussed in detail in Chapter Four.

While several studies have clearly demonstrated that there are race and gender differences on the AFOQT, it is critical to note that these differences are *average* group differences. The average differences do not speak to the performance of any specific individual belonging to any of the groups. For example, there are many black applicants who outperform many white applicants on the AFOQT. Similarly, there are women who outperform many men on the pilot composite. For this reason, the group differences cannot be used to draw conclusions about individuals within those groups. Many women and many minority applicants perform very well on the AFOQT.

It is worth noting that the observed average race and gender differences are very similar to those observed in the population outside the Air Force.[15] This effect could be mitigated by targeting higher-aptitude minorities and women, but those candidates are in high demand with all businesses hoping to attract them to their organization. Nevertheless, the fact remains that there are, on average, moderate-to-large group differences by race and gender for applicants taking the AFOQT.

---

[15] For a comparison to the magnitude of race and gender differences observed on other aptitude tests, see Chapter Four of this report.

Is the AFOQT a Biased Test?

When scores across race and gender groups differ as they do on the AFOQT, concerns about bias and unlawful discrimination naturally arise. However, *group differences in scores do not necessarily mean that a test is biased or discriminatory under the law.* The following sections clarify how group differences and bias are not equivalent concepts and summarize the existing research on bias on the AFOQT.

What Is Bias?

Bias is a term that has a very specific meaning in the employment test industry, in the scientific community, and in federal law. Although many in the broader public often conflate bias with group differences on tests, the two are independent concepts. Bias can occur when there are no group differences on a test, and a test can be free from bias even when there are large group differences in scores.

The *Standards for Educational and Psychological Testing* (AERA, APA, and NCME, 1999) provides a set of guidelines published and endorsed by the American Psychological Association, the National Council on Measurement in Education, and the American Educational Research Association to promote the ethical and sound use of tests. It is the repository of best practices that are referenced in the legal guidelines on discrimination—the "Uniform Guidelines on Employee Selection Procedure" (Equal Employment Opportunity Commission, 1978). The *Standards* note that bias on tests in general can be quantified by a variety of statistical techniques.[16] However, according to the *Standards*, "when tests are used for selection and prediction, evidence of bias or lack of bias is generally sought in the relationships between test and criterion scores for the respective groups" (p. 79). In other words, in a selection test context, bias occurs when scores on a test for one group predict future performance differently relative to another group (Cleary, 1968; Humphreys, 1952). Therefore, the most concerning type of statistical bias in an employment context is predictive bias.

Predictive bias is identified by examining regression lines.[17] To explain the concept of predictive bias, we provide three hypothetical figures. Figure 3.6 illustrates a regression line for a hypothetical selection test predicting later performance ratings. The regression line shows the predicted performance level for each score on the selection test. In other words, as illustrated in the figure, if an applicant scores a 60 on the selection test, we would predict that his or her score will be about a 6 on later performance ratings.

Figure 3.7 illustrates a hypothetical test that is biased against black applicants. In this example, a score of 60 on the selection test has a very different meaning for white versus black applicants. The test predicts that white applicants with a score of 60 on the selection test would score about a 4 on later job performance. But for black applicants with a score of 60, the test predicts about an 8 on later job performance. Using the line for all applicants (as we did in the previous example) would overpredict the later performance of a white applicant and underpredict the later performance of a black applicant. Because the regression line for all applicants underpredicts black

---

[16] These statistical techniques include examination of differential item functioning, differential test functioning, and regression slope and intercept differences.

[17] Typically bias is identified by regression equations predicting job performance using subgroup membership, the selection test score, and interaction terms between subgroup membership and the test score. Significant subgroup coefficients or interaction term coefficients indicate bias. See Lautenschlager, and Mendoza, 1986; also Nunnally and Bernstein, 1994.

Figure 3.6
Illustration of the Relationship Between a Hypothetical Selection Test and Later Job Performance

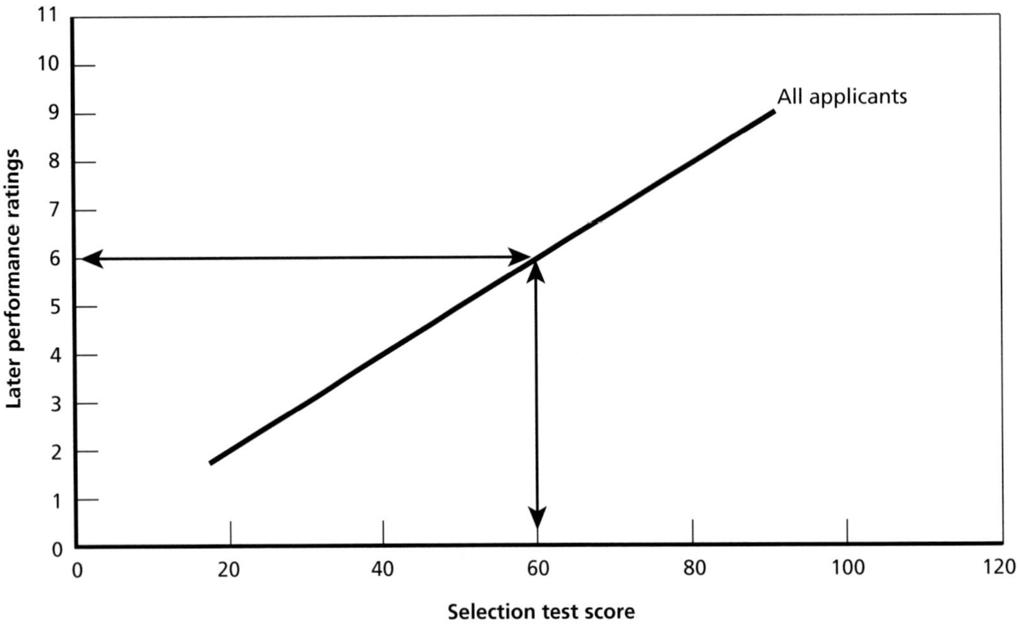

RAND *TR744-3.6*

Figure 3.7
Illustration of a Hypothetical Selection Test Biased Against Black Applicants

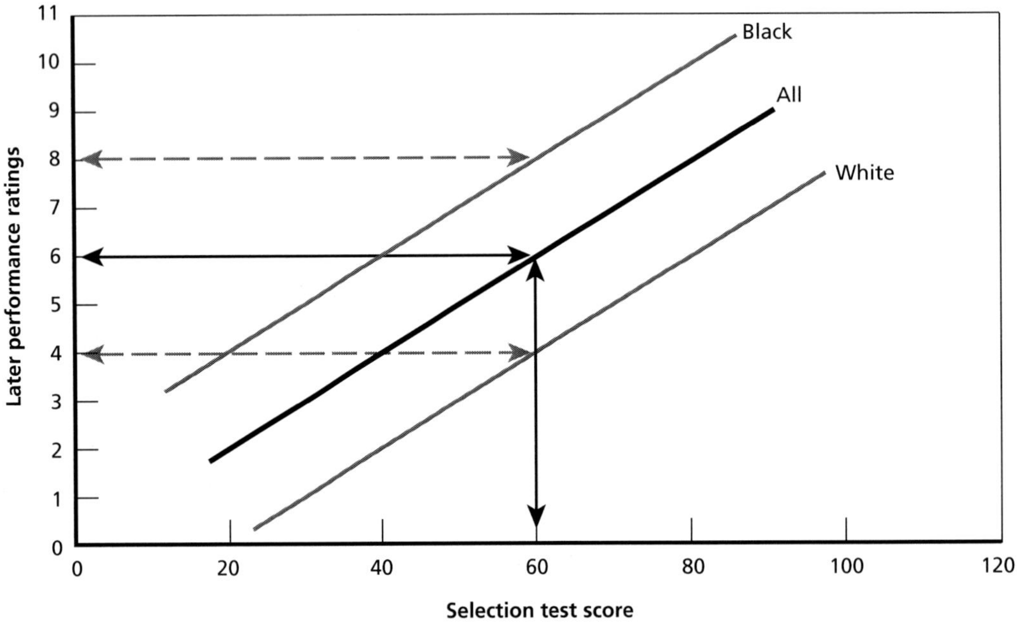

RAND *TR744-3.7*

performance and overpredicts white performance, it is biased against black applicants and it is biased in favor of white applicants.

Although the possibility of bias against black applicants does exist, we often observe the opposite on aptitude measures: bias in favor of black applicants (Maxwell and Arvey, 1993; Schmidt, 1988). In other words, when we examine performance on aptitude measures, we often observe the phenomena depicted in Figure 3.8.

In this figure, if we use the regression line for all applicants, white applicants' performance is underpredicted, and black applicants' performance is overpredicted.

The issue of underprediction as illustrated in these figures is the key to whether a test is biased against a particular group. However, it should be noted that, because there are so many groups to consider (e.g., black, Hispanic, Asian, and female applicants) a test that reduces underprediction for one important group often increases it for another (Ployhart and Holtz, 2008).

Studies of AFOQT Test Bias

Overall, investigations of bias on the AFOQT have not supported the conclusion that the AFOQT is biased against minorities and females. In fact, there is some evidence that the AFOQT may actually result in overprediction for black, Hispanic or female applicants (similar to the example in Figure 3.8), meaning the AFOQT might be biased in favor of those groups, if at all.

For example, Roberts and Skinner (1996) examined the relationship between AFOQT scores and final grades in officer training school for all trainees and then by race and gender.

Figure 3.8
Illustration of a Hypothetical Selection Test Biased in Favor of Black Applicants

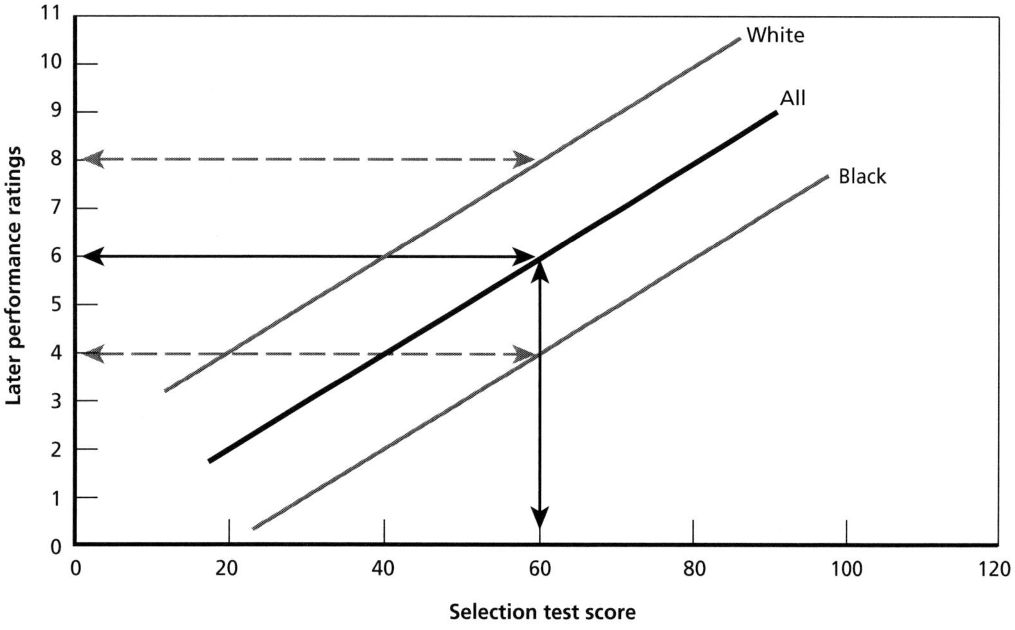

RAND *TR744-3.8*

They found that black trainees' scores in training were overpredicted. In that study, a score of 66.43 on the AFOQT academic composite yielded a predicted final course grade of 91.88 using the line for all students. However, using the regression line for the black trainees separately, the same AFOQT score (66.43) resulted in a predicted final course grade of 91.50. Thus, the regression line for all trainees overpredicted final course grades for black trainees by 0.38 points, showing bias in favor of black trainees. The AFOQT verbal and quantitative composite tests similarly overpredicted OTS final course grades for black Air Force trainees by 0.58 and 0.71 points, respectively. Among female Air Force trainees, the AFOQT academic, verbal, and quantitative composite tests were found to overpredict OTS final course grades by 0.52, 0.96, and 0.28 points, respectively.

Roberts and Skinner (1996) also examined bias in predicting officer training effectiveness reports; however, they found no evidence of bias against black trainees or female trainees in the AFOQT academic, quantitative, and verbal composites. Instead, the AFOQT quantitative composite was found to overpredict for black cadets. Among female Air Force trainees, the AFOQT quantitative and verbal composite tests both overpredicted effectiveness reports. Compared with OTS final course grades, the AFOQT showed much less overprediction of officer training effectiveness report performances.

Research examining bias in predicting pilot success has revealed similar findings. Carretta (1997) found no bias against black, Hispanic, or female applicants for predicting pilot training pass/fail scores. He did observe the typical overprediction for Hispanic and female scores.

Other studies examining predictive bias in the AFOQT in relation to completion of OTS have also showed that the AFOQT is not biased against minorities or women. Mathews (1977) found that the AFOQT overpredicted black OTS performance compared with white performance.

In sum, studies of the AFOQT have shown that the test is not biased against female, black, or Hispanic test takers.[18] Observed overprediction for minorities is consistent with many other tests of aptitudes and abilities and therefore is not unexpected. Nevertheless, as noted previously, bias is different from mean differences in test scores. As illustrated here, although there are very large differences in mean AFOQT scores between black applicants and white applicants, the AFOQT is not biased against black applicants.[19]

What Is Unlawful Discrimination?

Title VII of the Civil Rights Act of 1964 and the equal protection clause of the Fourteenth Amendment of the U.S. Constitution prohibit public employers from discriminating on the basis of race, color, religion, gender, and national origin. Title VII applies to civilian employees of the military; however, some courts have found that Title VII does not apply to military ser-

[18] Studies of the AFOQT have only examined bias against black, Hispanic, and female test takers; therefore, this statement does not imply that the test is biased against other groups that have been omitted (e.g., Native Americans). Rather, no conclusive AFOQT research has been published regarding bias against any other groups.

[19] Although an in-depth discussion of the possible causes (other than bias) for race or gender differences on the AFOQT is far beyond the scope of this report, it is worth noting that possible explanations include meaningful differences in candidates' education or experiences when growing up and the type of candidate who is attracted to, or recruited for, Air Force service or for specific aircrew positions. Such differences are not the fault of the test; however, they would be manifested in differences in test scores as well as in later success in certain Air Force jobs.

vicemembers as a matter of law.[20] Even so, the military generally applies the substantive rules of Title VII to military servicemembers as a matter of policy (and the Fourteenth Amendment applies to the military).

Title VII forbids several types of employment discrimination. They are generally divided into two types of discrimination: disparate treatment and disparate impact.[21] Disparate *treatment* occurs when members of a protected group (e.g., any race or gender) are not held to the same standards as any other protected group during the selection process. This includes using different selection tests, cut points, or selection procedures for different groups. With respect to the AFOQT, all applicants are required to meet the same cut scores and their scores are not otherwise altered; therefore AFOQT cut scores do not pose disparate treatment (42 U.S.C. §2000e-2(l)).

Disparate *impact* occurs when a facially neutral employment policy or practice has a significant adverse effect on members of a particular race, color, religion, gender, or national origin. However, just because a test has a disparate impact does not make it unlawful. Title VII shields employers from liability under disparate impact if they can demonstrate that "the challenged practice is job related for the position in question and consistent with business necessity" (42 U.S.C. §2000e-2(k)(1)(A)(i)).

To provide guidance to help employers comply with Title VII, the Equal Employment Opportunity Commission, the U.S. Departments of Labor and Justice, and the Civil Service Commission (now called the Office of Personnel Management) jointly promulgated the *Uniform Guidelines on Employee Selection Procedures.* According to these guidelines, disparate impact is considered to exist when the proportion of one protected group that is hired is less than four-fifths (80 percent) of the proportion hired from the protected group with the highest selection rate (usually white or male applicants).[22] This is often referred to as the *four-fifths rule.*

Because selection tests are used in many employment contexts and can cause disparate impact, employment selection test validation is one of the subjects on which the Uniform Guidelines provide specific guidance. Disparate impact usually occurs when there are mean protected group (e.g., race or gender) differences on tests and therefore is relevant for the AFOQT. However, *disparate impact as a result of a selection test is not considered illegal discrimination under the law if the selection test that caused it is a valid predictor of an important job-related outcome such as job performance.* In essence, a test that violates the four-fifths rule must establish evidence of validity or job-relatedness.[23] The Uniform Guidelines provide instructions on how to determine whether a selection test validly predicts a job-related outcome and is consistent with business necessity. If the test is indeed valid, and there is no equally effective but less discriminatory test, then the test does not violate Title VII.

The responsibility for designing selection tests and determining the validity and bias of selection tests falls upon professionals in the discipline of industrial/organizational psychology

---

[20] See Roper v. Dep't of Army, 832 F.2d 247, 248 (2d Cir. 1987); Gonzalez v. Dep't of Army, 718 F.2d 926, 928-29 (9th Cir. 1983); Taylor v. Jones, 653 F.2d 1193, 1200 (8th Cir. 1981).

[21] The Equal Protection clause covers disparate treatment but not disparate impact.

[22] Courts and federal enforcement agencies have also adopted other means of identifying disparate impact, such as the use of various measures of statistical significance.

[23] 42 U.S.C. §2000e-2(k)(1)(A)(i).

and closely related fields (e.g., educational psychology and organizational behavior). Professional practice in these disciplines is to follow the guidelines on test validity provided by the Uniform Guidelines. The research discussed in this report examined the AFOQT according to this professional practice. As members of these disciplines, we conclude that the studies described in this report indicate that the AFOQT is indeed a valid test as defined by the Uniform Guidelines. The AFOQT does show large differences between the average scores for several of the protected groups, which triggers further analysis under the four-fifths rule (EASI Consult, Schwartz, and Weissmuller, 2008).[24] However, because the AFOQT has been shown to have good validity for predicting important Air Force outcomes such as officer training and pilot training success, and previous empirical research regarding black, Hispanic, and female applicants demonstrates that the AFOQT is not biased against them, it is not considered discriminatory against those groups.

Is the AFOQT a Fair Test?

Bias and fairness are related but different concepts. Test fairness is based upon judgments of the appropriate and fair use of tests. Test fairness is not a statistically defined concept but rather a social policy concept that is subject to ever-changing individual and societal interpretations. Thus, definitions of test fairness are varied, and consensus on a single meaning of fairness has not been reached (for a review on definitions of test fairness see Arvey and Faley, 1988). Nevertheless, psychologists and test developers have agreed on several aspects of fairness as outlined in the *Standards for Educational and Psychological Testing* (AERA, APA, and NCME, 1999).

First, a fair test is one that is free from bias against particular groups (AERA, APA, and NCME, 1999). This is essentially the same as the legal concept of fairness as defined in the Uniform Guidelines (Equal Employment Opportunity Commission, 1978). Therefore, according to this definition, the AFOQT has been shown to be fair for those groups that have been investigated.

Second, a fair test is one that affords all test takers a comparable opportunity to demonstrate the abilities or attributes being measured by the test (AERA, APA, and NCME, 1999). This includes providing examinees with suitable testing conditions (e.g., standardized testing administration) and equal opportunities to prepare for the test (e.g., access to practice materials). If a test does not afford some groups the same opportunities to demonstrate their true abilities or attributes being measured by a test, it would likely result in a test that demonstrates bias against that group. This could potentially occur for non–native English speakers who take the AFOQT. The test would be unfair to them if they are not able to demonstrate their true ability because of their language difficulties, so long as those language difficulties would not affect their ability as officers, pilots, combat systems operators, or other aircrew personnel. We know of no study examining whether the AFOQT is biased against non–native English speakers.

Indeed, if individuals are randomly denied opportunities to demonstrate their true abilities or attributes as measured by a test, the test would not show bias against particular groups. Nevertheless, by this definition of fairness—namely, equitable treatment in the testing process—the test would still be considered unfair to individuals.

---

[24] It is important to note that this report does not examine how the Air Force actually uses AFOQT results or the Air Force's ultimate decisions regarding which applicants to accept.

Third, a fair test is one that offers everyone the same opportunity to learn the test material (AERA, APA, and NCME, 1999). Tests are often used to assess an examinee's knowledge of particular subject matter or skill attainment following formal instruction. Examinees who have not had the opportunity to learn the subject matter or to receive formal instruction in the area being tested often obtain low test scores. Thus, although low test scores may be indicative of a failure to learn, they may also reflect the lack of opportunity to learn the content or skills being assessed. The *Standards* (AERA, APA, and NCME, 1999) do note that opportunities to learn skills that can only be developed over many years play no role in the fairness of employment testing. In the case of the AFOQT, a majority of the subtests measure aptitudes that are developed only over a lifetime of learning.[25] For this reason, the verbal and quantitative composites would not be considered unfair under this definition of fairness. However, the *Standards* also note that in instances in which the employer provides materials for preparing for the test, the employer should ensure that those materials are made available to all applicants. Therefore, for purposes of fairness, any AFOQT preparation material prepared by the Air Force should be provided to all applicants. For example, the Air Force does provide an AFOQT information pamphlet, but this resource is not as well publicized as it could be.[26] To illustrate this point, a Google search for AFOQT information brought up a link to a description of the AFOQT on the official Air Force ROTC web page. On that web page (U.S. Air Force ROTC—Qualifying Test, 2009), the official AFOQT information pamphlet is not mentioned or provided. Instead, students are directed to "[c]heck out your local bookstore's test review section for commercial AFOQT test preparation guides." Barron's, Cliffs Test Prep, and Learning Express are some of the unofficial, commercial sources of AFOQT test preparation manuals available at bookstores.

Is the AFOQT a fair test? Based on the first definition of fairness, yes. Most of the research focused on the AFOQT has involved issues related to test bias and equality and can be summarized by saying that the AFOQT is not a biased test. Based on the other two definitions, there is little evidence to judge the fairness. We are not aware of any research on the fairness of the AFOQT in terms of equitable treatment of individuals in the testing process and equal opportunities for individuals to learn the material covered in the AFOQT. Nevertheless, these two remaining issues of fairness raise concerns not about the appropriateness of the test itself but rather about whether applicants have opportunities to review the test preparation materials and are provided with fair testing environments.

Does the AFOQT Make Mistakes in Prediction?

Selection tests are not perfect predictors of future success. In fact, there is significant error in the predictions made in all kinds of selection tests. Some applicants with high test scores do fail to perform well on the job, and other applicants with low test scores do perform very well on the job. While these mistakes in prediction invariably occur, they occur less often when using tests with high predictive validity than tests with low predictive validity.

When a selection test is valid, it means that with every increase in score, the likelihood of performing well on the job also increases. So someone with a score of 150 is more likely to

---

[25] Possible exceptions are the subtests used exclusively in the pilot composite. Specifically, aviation information and instrument comprehension subtests may include information and skills that could be learned in a short time, although no research has investigated whether or not this is true.

[26] See Department of the Air Force, *Officer Qualifying Test Information Pamphlet,* AFPT 997, n.d.

perform better on the job than someone with a score of 100. Based on this information, it is a better choice to hire the person who scores 150 than the person who scores 100. This is not to say that the person who scores 100 will not succeed on the job, just that it is less likely.

From the perspective of an individual who is rejected, this may seem unfair, especially if that individual would have performed well on the job. Although some individuals may be incorrectly classified (i.e., they would have done well on the job even though they had a lower test score) and thus have an unfair outcome even with the best selection system available, it is inappropriate to consider the fate of these few to be more important than the fate of the multitudes in the selection process. Moreover, if the alternative is to use a less-valid measure, the outcome would be less fair overall. Use of a less-valid measure would result in more prediction mistakes and in the inadvertent rejection of many more people who would have performed well on the job.

From the perspective of an organization that selects hundreds or thousands of applicants and spends a considerable amount of money training them, using the most-valid selection measure possible is not only fair but also consistent with best practices under the law and a prudent use of shareholder or taxpayer resources. Using the most-valid measure available ensures that the Air Force does not expend valuable resources training those who will not achieve as high a level of performance on the job on average or who will require substantially more training and experience to reach acceptable standards of performance. Another potential detrimental consequence of selecting less-qualified people is forcing other, higher-performing employees to compensate for lower performers, potentially making the job more stressful for the very employees that an organization would most desire to retain.

For any organization that is public in some fashion (i.e., supports itself with shareholder or taxpayer funds), this impetus to emphasize the fair outcome for many over the potentially unfair outcome for the few is even greater because the costs of poor prediction due to nonoptimal selection systems are borne by others, as well as by the organization itself. The flip side of this imperative is that the organization bears the responsibility, both for itself and for those who depend on its outputs, to design the best selection system possible and use it in an optimal fashion to minimize such classification mistakes.

Although selection tests do make mistakes, such mistakes become fewer as the validity of a test goes up. Therefore, the use of tests such as the AFOQT, which are known to have good validity for predicting Air Force outcomes, minimizes the number and severity of the selection mistakes. For this reason, the fact that the AFOQT does, on occasion, result in mistakes in prediction is not a reasonable argument for eliminating the test. Moreover, from the perspective of a large organization, such as the Air Force, that has many positions to fill, overall decreases in the number of selection mistakes on the aggregate far outweigh the claims of any one individual who has been misclassified.

Are There Less-Expensive Alternatives to Developing and Administering the AFOQT?

Test development, test administration, test security, and testing time all contribute to the overall cost of testing. The cost of developing and maintaining a personnel selection test can be quite high, and such costs are prohibitive for most organizations. Those organizations turn to other personnel selection measures that have been developed and maintained by a variety of testing organizations and consulting firms. Despite the fact that such testing can be outsourced, development costs will be incorporated into the costs of the test itself in one form or another. For some tests, such as the SAT and other academic entrance tests, the burden is borne primarily by the test takers as well as organizations such as the College Board, whose business is the development and maintenance of the SAT. For other tests, such as those used in the majority of employment contexts, the burden is borne by the hiring organizations.

The costs of development and administration of the AFOQT are borne by the Air Force. Contracts for the development of new test forms can run as much as $2 million.[27] Although there is no exact estimate of the day-to-day costs of administering the test to the thousands who apply for officer positions each year, the amount is certainly significant. Conversely, using the AFOQT to screen out candidates who will not be successful in training can result in large cost savings. For example, in an email communication on June 8, 2009, Johnny Weissmuller of AFPC estimated the amount of training money saved by using the AFOQT (or an equally valid measure) for screening pilots at approximately $5.9 million or more per year.[28] Nevertheless, the cost of the development and administration of the AFOQT is one reason that a similar measure, the SAT, has been considered as a replacement for the AFOQT. Chapter Four explores that issue in more detail.

Summary

Overall, the AFOQT is a useful test. Research shows that it has good validity for predicting training success in a wide variety of officer occupations and for predicting pilot training success. Although research has clearly and repeatedly shown that it is a fair test that is not biased against minorities or women, large and persistent race and gender group differences in scores remain. Given these large score differences, the AFOQT's use would result in a smaller proportion of minority individuals and women being selected into the officer corps than exists in the officer applicant pool. But such a reduction in diversity of selectees does not negate its importance as a valid selection tool for the Air Force.[29] The test is a valuable and unbiased predictor of who will succeed in officer training, without regard to race and gender.[30]

---

27 Telephone conversation with Kenneth Schwartz, October 9, 2008.

28 This estimate is conservative and narrowly focused. It is based only on gains from using the AFOQT pilot composite, and it accounted for only main-track pilot training (fighter/bombers and tanker/transport) cost savings (i.e., it did not consider training cost savings for pilots of unmanned aerial vehicles or special operations vehicles (helicopters, etc.) or combat system operators). Therefore, the full AFOQT offers even more potential for annual training cost savings in several additional Air Force specialties, if implemented.

29 See the Glossary for the definition of diversity as it is used in this report.

30 Note that the differences in AFOQT scores observed, on average, across race and gender groups provide no insight into the scores of any one individual who is a member of a given race or gender group. Even though minorities and women tend to score lower than white or male applicants, respectively, there are still many high-scoring individuals who are minorities and women. These high-scoring individuals would be predicted to do well as officers regardless of their race and gender.

CHAPTER FOUR

Should the SAT Replace the Air Force Officer Qualifying Test?

Concerns regarding the AFOQT's effect on diversity and the costs of developing and administering the AFOQT have prompted some to explore alternative measures to replace the AFOQT. One such measure is the SAT.

The SAT reasoning test (formerly the SAT I) is a standardized test that has been widely used for college and university admissions for many decades. The most recent version of the SAT assesses verbal reasoning with multiple-choice items and an essay and mathematical reasoning with multiple-choice items and numerical write-in answers. Total testing time is about four hours (College Board, 2009b). Scores on the verbal and math sections range from 200 to 800, and data on percentile rank corresponding to each score are reported as well.

Like the AFOQT, the SAT has undergone numerous revisions and changes over the years for a number of reasons, including cost, face validity, fairness, and public perception of the test (Lawrence et al., 2003). Changes are "intended to make the test more useful to students, teachers, high school counselors, and college admissions staff" (Lawrence et al., 2003, p. 1). Most recently, the SAT was changed in 2005 to include a 25-minute essay and to remove the verbal analogy items (College Board, 2009c).

Is the SAT a Valid Predictor?

As with the AFOQT, any potential replacement measure must be able to predict important Air Force outcomes. The SAT is primarily used in an academic context and thus most of the available evidence of its validity is in that context. However, that evidence, when coupled with the more-limited evidence that the SAT is also a valid predictor in the workplace context, suggests that the SAT may fulfill this validity requirement.

Predicting Academic Outcomes

The SAT was developed primarily as an indicator of college success. Thus, most of the research on SAT predictive validity has examined the prediction of college outcomes (Burton and Ramist, 2001). Hundreds of studies have shown that the SAT predicts college outcomes; however, an overwhelming majority of that research has mainly examined prediction of freshman GPA (Camara and Echternacht, 2000). For example, a recent study of 110 colleges (Kobrin et al., 2008) reported an average SAT validity of 0.35 for predicting freshman GPA. This finding is consistent with past research on validities from 1976 to 1985 that showed high validities for all years (Morgan, 1989), a summary of 99 validity studies showing that SAT validities are substantial and generalize across a variety of colleges (Bolt, 1986), and a review of numerous studies between 1930 and 1980 showing consistently strong validity for predicting first-year GPA (Wilson, 1983).

SAT scores have also been shown to predict college graduation and cumulative GPA. Across eight independent studies between 1980 and 1995, the average validity for predicting graduation was 0.33 (Burton and Ramist, 2001). With respect to cumulative GPA, which has been more widely studied, numerous studies also suggest that the SAT is a good predictor. For example, a recent review of 19 independent studies between the 1980s and mid-1990s reports an average validity of 0.36 (Burton and Ramist, 2001), and an earlier review of 32 studies between 1930 and 1980 (Wilson, 1983) yielded an average validity coefficient of 0.42 for predicting cumulative GPA.

Last, the SAT not only predicts college performance in general, it also predicts college success at the USAFA. More specifically, the SAT verbal and math subtests have been shown to predict first-year GPA in the USAFA for two cohorts of students (Lenning, 1975). Predictive validities were 0.35 and 0.45 for verbal and 0.40 and 0.47 for math.[1]

Predicting Work-Related Outcomes

In contrast to the large amount of research on SAT predictive validity regarding college outcomes, empirical studies examining the validity of the SAT for predicting important work-related outcomes are few. Nevertheless, there is some evidence that the SAT would be a good predictor of officer training success in the Air Force.

First, there is evidence that tests predicting success in college also predict success in work settings, regardless of the test's designed purpose. For example, Kuncel, Hezlett, and Ones (2004) found that test validity generalized from college settings to work settings—probably because the verbal and quantitative aptitudes needed to perform well in college are also needed in a variety of important work settings. Second, there is research indicating that the SAT demonstrates comparable validity to the AFOQT for predicting important Air Force outcomes. Cowan, Barrett, and Wegner (1989) examined SAT data on ROTC applicants between 1978 and 1981 and reported essentially identical SAT and AFOQT academic composite validities (see Table 4.1).

Other support for the possibility of replacing the AFOQT with the SAT comes from evidence showing that the SAT correlates highly with the AFOQT. For example, Diehl (1986) examined scores from 3,575 cadets entering the professional officer corps and found a correla-

Table 4.1
SAT and AFOQT Academic Composite Validities

Predicted Outcomes	SAT Validity	AFOQT Validity
Completion of the professional officer course	0.07	0.06
Distinguished graduate status	0.16	0.15
Instructor ratings of performance	0.12	0.12
Technical training course grades	0.39	0.37

SOURCE: Cowan, Barrett, and Wegner, 1989.

[1] These estimates were corrected for range restriction.

tion of 0.80 for SAT scores with the AFOQT academic composite (i.e., combined verbal and quantitative scores).[2] The math section of the SAT correlated more strongly with the AFOQT quantitative composite than with the verbal composite (0.71 and 0.47 respectively), and the verbal section on the SAT correlated more highly with the AFOQT verbal composite than with the quantitative composite (0.77 and 0.43 respectively). This shows that the SAT verbal and the AFOQT verbal measure similar aptitudes, and the SAT math and the AFOQT quantitative also measure similar aptitudes. But although the SAT does appear to measure similar verbal and quantitative aptitudes as the AFOQT, the SAT's relationships with the pilot and navigator composites (0.40 and 0.55 respectively) were not as strong, suggesting that the SAT cannot replace the pilot and navigator composites.

Ree and Carretta (1998) also explored the relationships between the SAT and the AFOQT verbal and quantitative subtests. Using data on 7,940 ROTC cadets, they reported correlations between the verbal SAT and AFOQT verbal composite scores and math SAT and AFOQT quantitative composite scores of 0.85 and 0.84 respectively.[3] They also demonstrated through a factor analysis of the results that the verbal and quantitative composites of the AFOQT and the SAT measure similar abilities. They concluded that the potential interchangeability of the SAT for the verbal and quantitative composites of the AFOQT is high, although it cannot be expected to replace the pilot and navigator composites, because of the uniqueness of those measures. In spite of their encouraging findings, Ree and Carretta noted that additional analyses are needed.

In further investigation of the interchangeability of the AFOQT and the SAT, Ree, Carretta, and Earles (2003) examined the statistical equivalence of scores on the AFOQT and the SAT and found evidence that SAT and AFOQT scores are equivalent overall but not within races and genders. Therefore, if one test were to be substituted for another, it would be critical to establish whether scores on the two tests were equivalent both overall and within protected groups (e.g., races and genders). These differential effects on race and gender groups raise concerns about whether the SAT could be used to replace the AFOQT.

Are There Group Differences on the SAT?

As discussed in Chapter Three, race and gender group differences on a selection test will reduce the race and gender diversity of those who are hired. The AFOQT has group differences in scores and hence does reduce diversity. However, to the extent that the SAT exhibits similar group differences, replacing the AFOQT with the SAT is unlikely to improve diversity. Unfortunately, SAT group differences are very similar to the differences on the AFOQT.

In one of the most comprehensive up-to-date reviews on SAT performance among college-bound seniors, Kobrin, Sathy, and Shaw (2007) provide evidence of persistent group differences across gender and ethnicity. Data drawn from 1987 through 2006 show that male students outperformed female students every year on both the SAT verbal and SAT math sections (Kobrin et al., 2008). Gender differences on the SAT verbal section were generally small

---

[2] No corrections for range restriction or unreliability in the criterion were applied; hence, these are conservative estimates that likely underestimate the true relationships.

[3] These correlations were corrected for range restriction.

($d = -0.12$ or less) compared with differences on the SAT math section (ranging from $d = 0.30$ to -0.39).[4] Their findings also revealed differences in average SAT verbal and mathematic scores across ethnic groups. On the SAT verbal section, students self-identifying as white obtained higher scores compared with all other ethnic groups during the 20-year period. In contrast, on the SAT mathematics section, Asian students outperformed all other ethnic groups. The next highest scoring group on the math section was the white student group, followed by the Native American/Alaskan Native, Hispanic, and black students. Over the past two decades, nearly all ethnic groups have exhibited score increases in both sections, with Asian and Native American students showing the largest gains while black and Hispanic students displayed more-modest improvements in scores.

Roth et al.'s (2001) meta-analysis of the differences between white scores and black and Hispanic scores on the SAT, ACT, and GRE are consistent with those findings. Table 4.2 shows their results with the magnitude of race differences in standardized units (*d*) compared with the results for the AFOQT.

As shown in Table 4.2, the race differences reported by Roth et al. (2001) are similar to those observed on the AFOQT. This suggests that the SAT would result in a roughly comparable reduction in diversity if the SAT were used to replace the AFOQT.

Is the SAT a Biased Test?

As discussed in Chapter Three, group differences are not an indication of bias in and of themselves, although they are a cause for further scrutiny of a test. Therefore, as part of determining whether the SAT is an adequate substitute for the AFOQT, the SAT should be examined for bias. This section presents the existing research on whether the SAT displays overprediction or underprediction for minorities and women.

In an extensive review, Young (2001) examined all published studies on SAT bias for predicting college performance over a 25-year period beginning in 1974. For women, Young found several studies demonstrating underprediction of college performance, indicating that the SAT is biased against women. Similar underprediction has been found in other studies since Young's review as well (see, for example, Mattern et al., 2008; Cullen, Hardison, and Sackett, 2004).

Young (2001) also found that the SAT consistently overpredicts college performance among black and Hispanic students. This overprediction indicates that the SAT is not biased against black and Hispanic students but rather biased in their favor. More-recent studies have found similar overprediction for black students (Cullen, Hardison, and Sackett, 2004; Mattern et al., 2008) and Hispanic students (Mattern et al., 2008).

With respect to Asian students, the results are mixed. Of six studies on Asian students, Young found two studies showing underprediction and four studies showing overprediction.

When the researchers for one study showing overprediction applied statistical corrections to adjust for variable grading practices, evidence for underprediction was also found. These conflicting results caused Young to acknowledge that firm conclusions regarding bias against

---

[4] *d* is the difference in standard deviation units. See the section in Chapter Three entited "Are There Group Differences in AFOQT Scores?" for more explanation of *d*.

Table 4.2
Average Standardized Differences on Verbal, Quantitative, and Academic Aptitude Tests

College Admissions Tests	Black-White *d*	Hispanic-White *d*
Verbal aptitudes		
AFOQT verbal	−0.88	−0.62
SAT verbal	−0.84	−0.70
ACT verbal	−0.92	−0.61
GRE verbal	−1.10	−0.60
Quantitative aptitudes		
AFOQT quantitative	−1.05	−0.57
SAT math	−0.90	−0.69
ACT math	−0.82	−0.35
GRE math	−1.08	−0.51
GRE analytical	−1.23	−0.71
Overall academic aptitudes		
AFOQT academic (verbal and quantitative)	−1.13	−0.69
SAT total	−0.97	−0.77
ACT total	−1.02	−0.56
GRE total	−1.34	−0.72

SOURCES: Data on SAT, GRE, and ACT reported in Roth et al., 2001. Data on AFOQT computed from means and SDs reported in EASI·Consult, Schwartz, and Weissmuller, 2008.

NOTE: *d* is the standardized difference between the corresponding group's mean and the white mean. It is calculated as the difference between the means divided by the average of the two standard deviations.

Asian students could not be established. A more-recent investigation of 2006 freshman GPAs (Mattern et al., 2008) showed slight underprediction for the verbal section and slight overprediction for the math section, with essentially no over- or underprediction for the overall SAT score. Basically, it appears that there is no consistent pattern of over- or underprediction for Asian students.

Consistent evidence of overprediction confirms that the SAT, like the AFOQT, is not biased against black and Hispanic students. In contrast, consistent evidence of underprediction suggests that the SAT is biased against women whereas the AFOQT is not. Although the evidence of bias against women is disconcerting, it is not clear whether the same overprediction would be observed if the SAT were used for Air Force selection. Because the SAT is designed to measure academic performance, research on SAT bias has examined bias only in the prediction of college success. There is no evidence that the SAT would underpredict women's training success or job performance in the Air Force. Nevertheless, the evidence regarding underprediction of the SAT for female academic performance does raise concerns about its adequacy as a substitute for the AFOQT.

Are There Other Concerns with Substituting the SAT for the AFOQT?

On the surface, there appear to be several advantages to using the SAT as a replacement for the AFOQT. First, with testing sessions available seven times per year at testing centers all across the United States (College Board, 2009b), the SAT is widely accessible to Air Force recruits. Second, unlike the AFOQT, which can only be taken twice, the SAT allows students to retake the test numerous times if they wish. Third, most officer applicants already have SAT scores (or ACT scores that can be converted to SAT scores), and therefore many applicants would not require additional testing. This would amount to significant cost savings for the Air Force. Fourth, the Air Force would not be required to shoulder the test development burden, also resulting in significant cost savings.

Nevertheless, there are significant problems in using the SAT instead of the AFOQT that would need to be addressed, many of which negate the advantages described above. First, the length of time between taking the SAT as a junior or senior in high school and applying for commissioning is commonly four to five years or higher in OTS and two to three years in ROTC, making the SAT a possibly dated indicator of current aptitude for many applicants, particularly those in OTS. This raises concerns about both validity and fairness. With respect to validity, it is possible that large time gaps between taking the SAT and application to the Air Force would result in lower validity than would be obtained if applicants were retested when they apply to the Air Force. Because there is some evidence that validity decreases as time since testing increases (e.g., Hulin, Henry, and Noon, 1990; Keil and Cortina, 2001), the utility of the SAT may be of concern for the Air Force.

With respect to fairness, it could be considered unfair to rely on outdated scores from tests taken years prior to application to the Air Force, particularly because wealthier applicants would be more willing to pay retesting costs to ensure that their scores are up-to-date. To curb this concern, the Air Force would have to consider covering the costs of SAT retesting at the time of application to the Air Force.

Second, the Air Force would not have control over test content, items, and scoring if the SAT were used in lieu of the AFOQT. The Air Force currently controls the content of the AFOQT such that the test measures the aptitudes predictive of performance as an officer. In contrast, the SAT is designed to measure achievement and reasoning in an academic setting. The SAT has undergone a number of changes over the years to address the criticisms and needs of the public and the academic community. For example, it recently faced a great deal of criticism from the public and specific challenges from the University of California (Lawrence et al., 2003). More specifically, some argue that the SAT should reflect curriculum-based achievement rather than general aptitudes (Atkinson, 2004). According to Lawrence et al. (2003), recent changes to the SAT "have been heavily influenced by a desire to reflect contemporary secondary school curriculum and reinforce sound educational standards and practices" (p. 11).

The Air Force's lack of control over the content of the test is a major drawback to switching to the SAT. As the SAT continues to evolve in future years to address concerns expressed by the educational community, its content may become less relevant for the Air Force community.

This could eventually result in lower validity, less fairness, and greater controversy over the Air Force's use of the SAT than there is now with the AFOQT.

Third, the Air Force would need to develop its own test norms for the SAT. Typically, test takers are high school juniors and seniors. As such, the SAT test population is noticeably different from the AFOQT test population, which ranges from high school seniors to college graduates. Essentially, the norm group used to determine SAT percentile scores is not applicable to Air Force applicants who complete the SAT. Development of new norms could be an expensive endeavor.

Fourth, as a selection tool, the SAT's three subtests offer less flexibility than the AFOQT. The Air Force currently modifies the relative contribution each of the eleven AFOQT subtests to optimally predict officer performance or performance in different aircrew jobs. In contrast, the SAT reports scores for only three tests: the math, verbal, and essay test; no additional subtest scores are available. This limits the flexibility of the SAT: Only three subscores could ever be included, excluded, or weighted as necessary for predicting officer performance—whereas the AFOQT has eleven.

Fifth, as noted above in the section on SAT validity, the SAT would not be as good as the AFOQT at predicting pilot, combat systems operator, or other aircrew training performance. This is likely because the AFOQT includes extra subtests (e.g., aviation knowledge and instrument comprehension) that are specially designed to predict pilot, combat systems operator, and other aircrew training success, which are not currently included in the SAT. Because selection of qualified pilots, combat systems operators, and other aircrew personnel is critical for the Air Force, it would be advisable to maintain a separate selection tool for that purpose. However, because eight of the eleven subtests on the AFOQT contribute to the pilot and navigator selection composites and five of those subtests have content not covered in the verbal and math sections of the SAT, about half of the AFOQT would still need to be maintained for pilot, combat systems operator, and other aircrew selection in the Air Force.[5] Therefore, if the Air Force continued to develop and use the subtests relevant for pilot, combat systems operator, and other aircrew selection, any reduction in development and testing costs due to using the SAT would be marginal at best.

Finally, a review of the evidence indicates that the SAT is subject to many of the same limitations that characterize the AFOQT. Specifically, as with the AFOQT, significant group differences have been found on the SAT. Black and Hispanic students on average obtain lower scores on the SAT than do white students. Similarly, women in general tend to score lower on the SAT than do men. Concerns about the ability to hire a racially diverse pool of officers would not be substantially alleviated by replacing the AFOQT with the SAT. Moreover, the evidence of underprediction of women's college performance for the SAT raises concerns that the SAT would be similarly biased for predicting important Air Force officer outcomes.

Summary

The disadvantages of using the SAT to replace the AFOQT appear to outweigh the benefits. If the Air Force were to use the SAT, the potential reduction in development and administration costs would also bring potential losses in validity for selecting pilots, combat systems operators,

---

5 See Table 2.1 in Chapter Two for a summary of which subtests contribute to the pilot and navigator subtests.

and other aircrew; no change in effects on diversity; and a test whose content may change in the future without regard for the Air Force's selection needs.

CHAPTER FIVE

Are There Any Other Tests That Could Be Used to Select Officers?

General aptitude tests (or cognitive ability tests), such as the AFOQT, have well-established validity. As delineated by Schmidt and Hunter (1998) in their review of selection research, there are multiple reasons why they should be considered the best selection tool. However, many other types of selection instruments have been shown to be valid predictors of performance (e.g., Hough and Oswald, 2000; Hunter and Hunter, 1984; Salgado, Viswesvaran, and Ones, 2002). Despite the many alternatives, not all selection tools are appropriate for selecting entry-level job applicants who have little prior experience in the job, as is typically the case of entry-level Air Force officers (officer candidates in OTS may be an exception). Examples of measurement tools that can be useful for entry-level selection include biodata (a measure of life experiences), interviews, and personality tests.

When examining selection tools, the *content* and *method* of the tool should be considered separately to the extent possible (Hunter and Hunter, 1984). Biographical data (biodata) interviews, and tests are all methods, while personality is a type of test content. Just as a test can measure a variety of content areas, interviews and biodata can also assess a variety of content areas, including personality, aptitude, and experience. In contrast, personality tests measure, by definition, personality. Nevertheless, interviews and biodata are often discussed with personality as alternatives to aptitude measures.

In the following sections we discuss these alternative selection measures and consider the use of selection systems that incorporate multiple selection tools.

Can the AFOQT Be Replaced by Measuring Relevant Life Experiences?

Biodata tools measure aspects of an applicant's life experiences. The items in a biodata tool are developed and selected with an eye to predicting work performance. There are conceptual rationales for what biodata tools measure and why those aspects of experience are important (e.g., Mael, 1991). However, as noted by Bliesener (1996), the nature of what biodata measures assess is not truly well defined.

Biodata tools have relatively high validity compared with other types of selection tools (e.g., Hunter and Hunter, 1984; Salgado, Viswesvaran, and Ones, 2002; Schmidt and Hunter, 1998). Hunter and Hunter (1984) note that biodata are second in rank only to aptitude measures in their validity for predicting the job performance of applicants with little prior job knowledge or experience. They note that the average validity of biodata is 0.37 compared with 0.53 for aptitude measures. The high validity of biodata is one reason the Air Force could consider using this type of tool, despite the fact that biodata more properly should be considered a method rather than a particular content area.

However, because the validity of biodata is nonetheless lower than that of aptitude tests, their use would likely represent a loss in the accuracy with which future job performance could be predicted if the test were used to replace the AFOQT. And using this method in addition to the AFOQT might not add much to prediction. As noted by Schmidt and Hunter (1998), biodata measures typically have a high correlation with aptitude measures, indicating a substantial amount of overlap in content.

Since biodata measures are not explicitly constructed to measure aptitude, it is not surprising that they are not the most reliable and valid measures of aptitude. Moreover, they still suffer some of the same diversity issues: The 2002 summary by Salgado, Viswesvaran, and Ones reports racial group differences on biodata measures, although the differences are smaller in size than those found for aptitude measures. For example, black scores were, on average, 0.33 standard deviations lower on biodata versus approximately 1.0 standard deviation lower on aptitude (Bobko, Roth, and Potosky, 1999). Evidence for gender differences on biodata tools is sparse, although it appears that these tools have a higher validity for women (0.51) than for men (0.27) (Bliesener, 1996).

Biodata tools also may be considerably more expensive to utilize than the AFOQT because the biodata tool itself would need to be developed. Relevant experiences that predict Air Force officer, pilot, combat systems operator, and other aircrew performance would need to be hypothesized and the items that tap these experiences developed. The instrument would then have to be tested for validity and refined. At the end of this expensive process, group differences might still be found (Hunter and Hunter, 1984, discuss some of the feasibility issues with regard to biodata).

Another downside to biodata measures is the possibility of coaching. Because biodata measures ask about people's past experiences, test takers can be taught to provide ideal responses rather than an honest representation of their true past experiences. A number of test coaching companies provide coaching materials for the AFOQT, though at present the material on the tests (e.g., math and verbal questions) is hard to fake. In contrast, biodata would be much easier to falsify. A biodata measure could include a lie scale to detect those who are attempting deceit; however, the only way to know with certainty whether respondents are being honest on such a measure would be to investigate the veracity of their claims. This would also be a costly endeavor.

Can the AFOQT Be Replaced by an Interview?

The interview is the most frequently used selection tool in the world (Salgado, Viswesvaran, and Ones, 2002). Interviews come in two major forms: structured, in which the content of the interview is explicitly defined prior to the interview, and unstructured, in which the content of the interview is not constrained. As Campion, Palmer, and Campion (1977) note, structured interviews are consistently found to be superior to unstructured interviews. Schmidt and Hunter (1998) report validities of 0.51 for structured interviews and 0.38 for unstructured interviews. The validity for structured interviews is clearly superior, although it can vary depending on the interview content and the degree and type of interview structure (e.g., see the review by Salgado, Viswesvaran, and Ones). However, although this validity estimate is equivalent to that reported by Schmidt and Hunter for aptitude tests, there are several issues to consider.

As with biodata, interviews are a method rather than a tool for assessing a particular content area. Indeed, as with biodata, structured interviews can have substantial content overlap with cognitive aptitude (Huffcutt, Roth, and McDaniel, 1996), although this overlap decreases on average with the degree of structure. Overlap also may be dependent on type of structure. For example, Huffcutt et al. indicate that behavioral-description-structured interviews, in which applicants are asked to describe past behaviors that are relevant to the desired job, have the lowest overlap with aptitude. This may present some complications for the construction of an interview for use in the current selection context, as some types of interviews (e.g., behavioral-description-structured interviews) are most applicable to candidates with job-relevant experience and hence inappropriate for entry-level selection use. A focus on the content of an interview rather than simply the method is also critical to ensure that the test has predictive validity and does not tap the same content as the AFOQT.

Despite these caveats, Huffcutt and Roth (1998) indicated that black-white group differences were smaller for interviews than those typically found for pure measures of cognitive aptitude (on average, black interviewees score about 0.25 standard deviations lower than white interviewees on interviews versus approximately 1 standard deviation lower for aptitude). The 2002 review of interview research by Salgado, Viswesvaran, and Ones indicated that evidence for gender group differences on interviews was inconclusive.

It does appear that structured interviews are currently in use for the selection of officers in the Air Force, although the degree and type of structure, as well as the content, is unclear. In addition to the simple administration of the interview questions, interviews need to be evaluated based on a scoring system to ensure consistency across interviewers and render the data easily accessible to decisionmakers. It is also unclear whether one system is used across accession sources or if there are multiple systems (see Ingerick, 2006, for additional detail).

Interviews and scoring systems must be validated, just as other types of selection tools are. It appears that this requirement is outstanding for the current interview systems used in the Air Force (Ingerick, 2006). Content overlap with aptitude and group differences for the existing interviews could be investigated empirically as part of the overall validation process. If the existing interviews and scoring systems are not identical across accession sources, as it appears they may not be, they would need to be validated separately.

If the Air Force were to employ the interview as a valid selection tool, it would incur significant expense for a number of essential steps, including development or investigation of structured interview content, development or refinement of a scoring system, validation of the overall interview process, and training interviewers. These steps are needed not just for development of a new interview, but also for retaining the current interview or interviews as part of a valid selection system. The costs of administration and scoring are greater for an interview than for an aptitude test like the AFOQT. Moreover, creation or modification of a valid structural interview will not necessarily meet the goal of obtaining validity as high or higher than that of the AFOQT while also reducing group differences. It is unlikely that an interview can be used to replace the AFOQT, and exploring the possibility via intensive development is likely to be very expensive.

Can the AFOQT Be Replaced by a Personality Test?

A third type of selection tool often considered is a personality test. Personality includes many dimensions, although much of the research dealing with personality at work has focused on the five-factor model of personality (Hough and Ones, 2002). This model describes personality in terms of five dimensions: extroversion/introversion, emotional stability/neuroticism, agreeableness, conscientiousness, and openness to experience. Although the names and directionality of the dimensions may vary somewhat depending on the specific test, these five dimensions are the ones most often used in selection contexts. Of the five personality traits, conscientiousness and extroversion are the best predictors of job performance, and their use in selection is well supported. The average validity of conscientiousness for predicting performance in all types of jobs is 0.18 (Ployhart and Holtz, 2008); for predicting performance specifically in managerial jobs, it is 0.22 (Barrick and Mount, 1991). Extroversion is also a good predictor of managerial performance; there, the average estimates of validity is 0.18 (Barrick and Mount, 1991). Other personality traits do not demonstrate such consistently high validities or, in the case of compound constructs, may show potential but do not have a substantial research literature supporting them.

A second main type of personality assessment used in work settings focuses specifically on personality aspects that are useful in the prediction of behavior at work. Integrity tests and drug and alcohol scales fall under the rubric of specific-focus personality tests (e.g., Salgado, Viswesvaran, and Ones, 2002) and are essentially combinations of the five-factor model traits of conscientiousness, agreeableness, and emotional stability/neuroticism (Hough and Ones, 2002; Ones, Viswesvaran, and Schmidt, 1993; Salgado, Viswesvaran, and Ones, 2002). Based on the relatively high average validities of 0.41 reported for integrity tests (Ones, Viswesvaran, and Schmidt, 1993), these tests are well supported for use in selection as well.

An important question, of course, is whether or not personality tests show group differences. Salgado et al. noted that the primary group differences investigated for personality scales are gender differences. Hough, Oswald, and Ployhart (2001) report small mean differences with women scoring higher on conscientiousness and lower on extroversion than men (d = 0.08 and –0.09, respectively). Women tend to score slightly higher than men on integrity tests (d = .16), a difference larger than any of those on the five factors individually. Hough, Ones, and Ployhart (2001) also report small racial/ethnic group differences across several groups for integrity tests, extroversion, and conscientiousness. The largest mean difference on any of the five factors and integrity tests was 0.21 for openness to experience (black scores were lower than white scores); mean differences were typically less than 0.10.

Although personality validities are not as high as general aptitude validities and hence their usefulness as a predictor of Air Force pilot performance is necessarily less, conscientiousness, extroversion, and integrity tests offer promise for use in selection in the current context. Nonetheless, as indicated previously, personality tests have lower validity than aptitude tests, so replacing the AFOQT with a measure of personality would invariably lead to more errors in the prediction of the success of Air Force officer applicants. However, because the content of personality measures do not overlap with aptitude measures, they could be a useful supplement to the AFOQT. The Air Force is already making progress toward integrating a personality assessment based on the five-factor model into its officer selection systems, in addition to the AFOQT aptitude measures. Currently under development is a new subtest of the AFOQT called the Self-Descriptive Inventory (SDI+), which is a measure of the five personality factors and two additional compound traits (Ingerick, 2006).

One major concern with these (and other) personality constructs is that they are susceptible to faking. That is, respondents may be able to identify the "correct" (e.g., high conscientiousness, high integrity) answer and therefore may opt to present themselves in a more positive light. Personality items are generally self-reported: An individual is asked to agree or disagree with statements that cannot be corroborated (e.g., they are asked how accurately on a scale of 1 [very inaccurate] to 5 [very accurate] a particular descriptor such as "Am always prepared" reflects their behavior [Goldberg et al., 2006]). The SDI+ is a self-report test and is subject to similar concerns (Ingerick, 2006).

Hough and Ones (2002) cite evidence indicating that, when people are instructed to do so, they can answer such self-report items in a way that makes them appear substantially better than those who are asked to answer items honestly. However, Hough and Ones also summarize the extensive research on this issue and indicate that data from applicant samples (i.e., respondents who have a reason to "fake good") show only slightly lower validities than data obtained from job incumbents in research settings (i.e., respondents who do not need to "fake good"). Morgeson et al. (2007) offer a more recent summary of the issues surrounding distortion and personality tests in a selection context and come to a similar conclusion. Thus, the predictive power of personality tests does not appear to be greatly affected by the motivation of applicants to appear in the most positive light to potential employers.

Nevertheless, personality tests are not typically used as high-stakes standardized tests that are administered to many thousands of applicants (as in the selection of Air Force officers). In high-stakes standardized testing contexts, concerns are less about applicants presenting themselves in a positive light (i.e., faking) and more about employing specialized coaching in order to perform well on the test. More specifically, there are a number of test coaching firms whose primary goal is to teach applicants to perform well on the AFOQT. If personality measures were added to the Air Force selection test battery, coaching firms would also add personality to their coaching repertoire. Although applicant faking on the test does not seem to affect the overall validity of the measures in regular employment contexts, coaching by test preparation companies could. There is some indication from research conducted by the U.S. Army (see White, Young, and Rumsey, 2001) that coaching is a particular concern in a similar military selection context and these concerns have derailed initial attempts to include personality and biodata measures in the selection system. However, management techniques and alternate forms of assessment are under investigation and bear promise (White, Young, and Rumsey, 2001), although further research is needed before a personality test could be considered a viable and fair selection instrument for the Air Force.

Can Other Tools Be Used in Combination with the AFOQT?

As noted by Schmidt and Hunter (1998) in their review of 85 years of selection research, there is simply no replacement for general aptitude in the selection context. Our consideration of some of the more-promising alternative selection tools here cannot contradict that conclusion: General cognitive aptitude has consistently demonstrated the highest validity in the initial job-entry selection context. An aptitude measure such as the AFOQT should not be replaced by any of the nonaptitude alternatives. However, other types of predictors may be used *in addi-*

tion to a cognitive ability measure in order to augment the prediction of job performance. This approach of combining measures with the AFOQT requires consideration of the predictive power contributed by other selection tools over and above that contributed by aptitude. Using other predictors in conjunction with aptitude, especially ones that do not demonstrate group differences, also offers the potential to decrease group differences in the selection process without a corresponding decrease in validity.

Of the above-reviewed selection tools, only personality tests clearly represent assessment of a different content area rather than a different selection method. Therefore, we will focus primarily on the usefulness of personality tests (specifically, integrity tests and the facet of conscientiousness) as an addition to a selection system that incorporates a test of general mental aptitude such as the AFOQT.

Ackerman and Heggestad (1997) provide evidence that the relationship between general aptitude and personality factors are typically small. When two predictors have a weak relationship (i.e., they have little content overlap) and both assess content related to relevant aspects of performance, then the two predictors are complementary and their combination will have higher overall validity than either one has alone. This is true of personality and aptitude: While aptitude is a known predictor of task performance on core job activities (see, e.g., Schmitt et al., 2003), personality constructs are shown to be related to different but still important aspects of performance, such as a tendency to put forth effort and to do things that, while not intrinsic to the work tasks themselves, support the completion of those tasks (this aspect of job performance is known as *contextual performance* [Borman and Motowidlo, 1993; Hough and Ones, 2002]).

A small relationship between such predictors as aptitude and conscientiousness or integrity has a positive implication for adding to the validity of the selection system: The overall increase in validity is likely to be larger when the predictors have weaker relationships (Schmidt and Hunter, 1998). As reported by Schmidt and Hunter, integrity tests have one of the highest validities over and above that of aptitude when they are used together in a selection context (an increase in validity of 0.14). Conscientiousness also demonstrates a relatively large increase in validity when used together with aptitude tests (0.09).

Ployhart and Holtz (2008) reviewed the research on the trade-off between the validity of a selection system as a whole (i.e., all the tests and procedures used for selecting applicants and how they are combined) and adverse impact. They described several strategies that organizations might use in an attempt to achieve both goals. One such strategy calls for using a valid and reliable personality test that measures integrity or conscientiousness in addition to a valid and reliable measure of aptitude. They found this to be the most effective strategy that does not result in a loss of predictive validity: It assesses the full range of knowledge, skills, abilities, and other characteristics that are required for job performance.

As noted, research indicates that personality tests may predict different yet relevant aspects of performance and hence increase the amount of performance content that is assessed by the tools in the selection system. Personality is, of course, not the only type of test that may be incorporated into the selection systems of the Air Force officer accession sources to complement the information provided by the AFOQT. For example, validated interviews that measure other important job-relevant content offer the potential to improve predictions of who will excel as an Air Force officer, with fewer of the concerns about coaching that plague personality tests.

Regardless of which alternatives are selected to supplement the AFOQT, it is worth noting again that aptitude measures should not be replaced with less-valid measures simply to improve diversity. To do so would be tantamount to sacrificing the quality of all selected officers. Minority and female officers, as well as white male officers, would be less likely to be successful on the job—producing a less effective Air Force in general.

Summary

As illustrated by Sackett and Ellingson (1997), there are limitations to the reductions in adverse impact that may be obtained when a valid selection system is sought. Nonetheless, inclusion of selection tools that add predictive power to the selection system and better capture multiple aspects of job performance is a useful approach (Ployhart and Holtz, 2008; Sackett, Borneman, and Connelly, 2008; Sackett et al., 2001). Moreover, researchers have suggested how best to weight the importance of multiple predictors in a selection system to minimize adverse impact without an appreciable sacrifice in the validity of the selection system (see De Corte, Lievens, and Sackett, 2007, for a useful tool for obtaining optimal trade-offs).

CHAPTER SIX

Conclusions

At the beginning of this report, we stated that we would address four questions. In response to the first question, "What is the AFOQT?" we described the AFOQT as a multiple-choice aptitude test that was developed by the Air Force and used as part of the officer selection system. Our conclusions regarding the remaining questions are each addressed in turn below.

The AFOQT Is a Valuable and Useful Test

Our second question was "Is the AFOQT a valuable and useful test?" Existing research on AFOQT validity and bias supports continued use of the AFOQT. The AFOQT has been shown to be a valid selection test for predicting training success in a variety of Air Force officer jobs. Studies of AFOQT bias show that the test is not biased against Hispanic, black, or female applicants. The fact that the test is not biased against those groups and is a valid predictor of important Air Force outcomes is a strong argument in favor of continued use of the AFOQT.

While past research does strongly support the conclusion that the AFOQT is a good selection test for the Air Force, two cons to its continued use are the cost of maintaining and refining the AFOQT and its impact on diversity. However, the cost of maintaining the AFOQT is not prohibitive. One estimate for test development costs is $2 million every eight years.[1] While this is not a paltry sum, it is relatively inexpensive in light of the cost of Air Force personnel initiatives more generally.

Diversity is the second major con to keeping the AFOQT. Despite its lack of bias, the AFOQT does have noticeable average race and gender differences. These differences result in a larger proportion of women and minorities being rejected relative to white and male applicants, which in turn leads to a less-diverse workforce. Although the reduction in diversity is no different than what is typically observed on other aptitude measures, the AFOQT is not an effective tool for increasing diversity.

The SAT Is Not an Ideal Replacement for the AFOQT

The third question we addressed was "Should the SAT replace the AFOQT?" Some have suggested substituting another measure of aptitude, such as the SAT, for the AFOQT as a way to maintain a valid selection system while increasing diversity. There is research demonstrating

1 Telephone conversation with Kenneth Schwartz, October 9, 2008.

that the verbal and quantitative composites of the AFOQT are very similar to the aptitudes and abilities measured on the SAT. For this reason, it is possible that the SAT could be a viable replacement for the verbal and quantitative composites on the AFOQT. Advantages to replacing the AFOQT with the SAT include reducing the Air Force's test development and administration costs and using a valid test that many applicants to Air Force officer accession sources already will have taken in the course of their academic careers.

Conversely, there are several reasons why the SAT is not a suitable replacement for the AFOQT. First, although aptitude tests such as the SAT and AFOQT are consistently valid predictors of job success (Schmidt and Hunter, 1998), the predictive power of such tests may decline as time passes and potential applicants have the opportunity to accumulate relevant training and experience (Keil and Cortina, 2001). Thus, the predictive power of an SAT score taken prior to entering the Air Force Academy or a college or university with an ROTC program is not likely to be as large as the predictive power of a test taken just prior to officer training. Therefore, for fairness purposes, the Air Force would need to retest applicants who took the SAT one or more years in the past.

Second, the pilot and navigator composites include some subtests, such as instrument reading and aviation knowledge, that could not be replaced by the SAT. Because these subtests add to the predictive power for selection of applicants who will be successful in pilot, combat systems operator, and other aircrew training, the validity over and above the validity contributed by aptitude would be lost if the AFOQT were replaced by the SAT. For this reason, the Air Force would still need to continue development and administration of those subtests for use in pilot, combat systems operator, and other aircrew selection. Thus, the need to maintain the pilot and navigator composites negates one of the reasons proposed for switching to the SAT—namely, reduced cost for development and administration. Given the need to continue development and administration of much of the AFOQT to maintain these composites, the cost savings in switching to the SAT would be minimal.

A third drawback to replacing the AFOQT with the SAT is lack of Air Force control over test content. The SAT was developed and used primarily for selection in educational settings. Therefore, improvements and changes to it are driven by the needs of educational institutions. As those needs evolve, the content of the test will likely change as well. As new sections are added and old sections are removed, the test would need to be revalidated for its compatibility with the Air Force's goals. This is of particular concern because revisions to the SAT would be intended to better emulate skills needed to succeed in an academic setting rather than the workplace.

Finally, replacing the AFOQT with the SAT (or another similar aptitude measure) would not achieve the goal of increasing diversity in the Air Force population. Valid measures of aptitude invariably show fairly large group differences in test scores, and such differences result in different rates of selection such that fewer minorities and women are selected. The SAT is no exception to this rule.

While we do not advise replacing the AFOQT with the SAT, it could be used instead of the AFOQT in certain preplanned circumstances. For example, for high school seniors applying to the Academy, the SAT is a sensible selection tool. It is a valid tool designed specifically for making college or university admissions decisions, and it is used for that purpose by many colleges and universities across the country. We, therefore, support its continued use for that purpose at the Academy. Given the high correlation between the SAT and the quantitative and verbal subtests of the AFOQT and the high entrance standards at the Academy, it would be unlikely that an Academy graduate who met the minimum SAT requirements for admissions to the Academy would not also meet the minimum AFOQT requirements for commissioning. Similarly, in evaluating the academic potential of high school ROTC applicants for awarding of ROTC scholarships, the SAT, which was designed for predicting the academic potential of college-bound high school students, is an ideal screening tool. ROTC currently accepts SAT scores for high school students applying for scholarships but only AFOQT scores for college students who are applying for scholarships. ROTC could consider accepting SAT scores instead of AFOQT scores for scholarship applications from students who are currently in college. It is worth noting, however, that for reasons of fairness students should be encouraged to provide a current SAT score if their original SAT scores produced during high school are not high enough to qualify for the scholarship. In other words, applicants should be permitted to retest to show their current (rather than outdated) qualifications. Note that if the testing requirement for all ROTC scholarship applications is changed to the SAT, those applicants who do not receive scholarships and instead wish to apply for commissioning without a scholarship and those applicants who are interested in pursuing specific air crew jobs (e.g. pilots) would still need to take the AFOQT.

Another circumstance where existing high school SAT scores could suffice in lieu of the AFOQT would be in instances where someone's SAT scores are sufficiently high enough (e.g., at the 90th percentile on the SAT) that he or she would almost certainly meet the minimum commissioning requirements on the AFOQT (set at only the 10th and 15th percentiles). Note that we do not currently know at what level scores on the SAT would be "sufficiently high enough" to be considered in place of the AFOQT. Some research suggests that the AFOQT and SAT may require subgroup-specific equipercentile weighting, which would argue against an easy crosswalk of scores (Ree, Carretta, and Earles 2003); however, setting a sufficiently high level for the SAT would potentially render such methodological questions a moot point. Nonetheless, to answer the question of what score level is "sufficiently high," a study would need to be conducted to identify the exact minimum score required to ensure, with a prespecified degree of confidence, that an individual's corresponding scores on the AFOQT would meet the minimum requirements for commissioning. Regardless of where that level is determined to be, there will be many people whose SAT scores fall below that prespecified level. Therefore, many applicants would still need to take the AFOQT. Moreover, any applicant considering a pilot or Combat Systems Officer position would also need to complete the AFOQT to obtain scores on the pilot composite. This illustrates how we advise that SAT be used: namely, as a replacement for the AFOQT *only* in limited circumstances.

Other Ways to Improve Prediction Are Available

The fourth question addressed in the report was "Are there any other tests that could be used to select officers?" In discussing replacement of the AFOQT with the SAT, we ascertained that aptitude is one of the most powerful predictors of later performance and hence one of the most useful; therefore, retaining some aptitude measure is essential. The Air Force has a good aptitude measure in the AFOQT. As described in Chapter Five, other tools may be a useful addition to the Air Force officer selection system. Although aptitude is a powerful predictor of job performance, the Air Force's selection system would benefit from the addition of other measures that predict multiple aspects of job performance (Ployhart and Holtz, 2008; Sackett, Borneman, and Connelly, 2008; Sackett et al., 2001).

The best approach to retain high validity in a selection system while also increasing diversity is to include aptitude measures along with additional measures, such as personality, that predict performance but do not show group differences (Ployhart and Holtz, 2008). Although there can be some negative impact on validity when attempting to minimize group differences (Sackett and Ellingson, 1997; Ployhart and Holtz, 2008), this would be the most feasible and potentially least expensive option available to the Air Force for increasing diversity.

Some Issues Remain

The selection systems currently used by the Air Force officer accession sources utilize a valid and strong predictor of officer performance, the AFOQT. However, the effectiveness of this tool is limited by the use of cut scores rather than the full range of scores. Using the full range of scores, in addition to other selection tools, is one way in which the prediction of Air Force officer success can be improved. Another important step is to ensure that the tools used in addition to the AFOQT are valid predictors of success in Air Force jobs. Some of the other selection tools currently used by the accessions sources (e.g., interviews and Relative Standing Scores) may not have been validated (Ingerick, 2006). Any part of the selection process used for selecting officers should be validated. In addition to its components, the Air Force officer selection system requires validation as a whole. Although individual parts may be valid, only validation of the entire system will lead to any certainty that the Air Force is using the most effective and fair selection system possible.

Policy Recommendations

Use the AFOQT to Its Fullest and Pursue Other Options for Increasing Diversity

Increasing officer diversity should continue to be a valued goal for the Air Force, but the goal of achieving diversity should not come at the expense of selecting qualified candidates. Because the AFOQT is a valid predictor of success in Air Force jobs, it should continue to be used for selecting officers and candidates for aircrew jobs. Efforts to increase diversity of officers should be directed at recruiting better-qualified minority and female candidates, not at eliminating a useful and valuable selection test. Replacing a valid and powerful predictor, such as the AFOQT, with a less-valid predictor to improve diversity is neither a necessary nor an acceptable alternative. Instead, valid measures that do not show group differences should be investigated to supplement the AFOQT.

Validate the Entire Officer and Aircrew Selection System

The AFOQT is just one piece of the overall officer and aircrew selection system. To achieve the goals of selecting the most-qualified applicants, the entire selection system should be examined for adverse impact and validated. The AFOQT should not be the only component of the selection system that is subject to scrutiny.

Identify New Selection Tools to Supplement the Validity of the Overall Selection System

New selection tools (such as personality, biodata measures, and structured interviews) could be added to the selection system to improve selection accuracy and possibly produce marginal increases in diversity. Such measures should be explored as possible supplements to the AFOQT in the current selection system. To do this, research studies on such experimental measures should be conducted to examine their usefulness in the Air Force context. Studies on coaching and faking should be conducted in the Air Force to examine the possible impacts on the fairness and validity of the experimental selection tools, and predictive validity and adverse impact studies should also be undertaken.

References

42 U.S.C. 21, *Civil Rights Act of 1964,* Title VII, Subchapter VI, §2000e.

Ackerman, P. L., and E. D. Heggestad, "Intelligence, Personality, and Interests: Evidence for Overlapping Traits," *Psychology Bulletin*, Vol. 121, 1997, pp. 219–245.

AERA, APA, and NCME—*See* American Educational Research Association, American Psychological Association, and National Council on Measurement in Education.

AFPC—*See* Air Force Personnel Center.

Air Education and Training Command (AETC), Instruction 36-2002, *Recruiting Procedures for the Air Force,* Randolph Air Force Base, Tex.: Headquarters, Air Force Recruiting Service, Enlisted Programs Management Branch (HQ AFRS/RSOP), August 18, 1999.

Air Force Instruction 36-2005, *Appointment in Commissioned Grades and Designation and Assignment in Professional Categories—Reserve of the Air Force and United States Air Force,* Washington, D.C.: Department of the Air Force, May 19, 2003.

Air Force Instruction 36-2013, *Officer Training School (OTS) and Enlisted Commissioning Programs (ECP)*, Washington, D.C.: Department of the Air Force, July 11, 2006.

Air Force Personnel Center (AFPC) Interactive Demographic Analysis System (IDEAS) report builder. Data downloaded as of May 21, 2009:
http://w11.afpc.randolph.af.mil/vbin/broker8.exe?_program=ideas.IDEAS_default.sas&_service=prod2pool3&_debug=0

American Educational Research Association, American Psychological Association, and National Council on Measurement in Education, *Standards for Educational and Psychological Testing,* Washington, D.C.: American Psychological Association, 1999.

Arth, First LT T. O., *Validation of the AFOQT for Non-Rated Officers*, Manpower and Personnel Division, File 11-2-1, Brooks AFB, Tex.: January 1986.

Arvey, R. D., and R. H. Faley, *Fairness in Selecting Employees*, 2nd ed., Reading, Mass.: Addison-Wesley, 1988.

Atkinson, R. C., "Achievement Versus Aptitude in College Admissions," in R. Zwick, ed., *Rethinking the SAT: The Future of Standardized Testing in University Admission*, New York, London: Routledge-Falmer, 2004, pp. 15–23.

Autor, D., and D. Scarborough, "Does Job Testing Harm Minority Workers? Evidence from Retail Establishments," *Quarterly Journal of Economics*, Vol. 1, No. 123, November 2008, pp. 219–277.

Barrick, M. R., and M. K. Mount, "The Big Five Personality Dimensions and Job Performance: A Meta-Analysis," *Personnel Psychology*, Vol. 44, 1991, pp. 1–26.

Bliesener, T., "Methodological Moderators in Validating Biographical Data in Personnel Selection," *Journal of Occupational and Organizational Psychology*, Vol. 69, 1996, pp. 107–120.

Bobko, P., P. L. Roth, and D. Potosky, "Derivation and Implications of a Meta-Analytic Matrix Incorporating Cognitive Ability, Alternative Predictors, and Job Performance," *Personnel Psychology*, Vol. 52, 1999, pp. 561–589.

Bolt, R. F., *Generalization of SAT Validity Across Colleges*, New York: The College Board, Report No. 86-3, 1986.

Borman, W. C., and S. J. Motowidlo, "Expanding the criterion domain to include elements of contextual performance," in Neal Schmitt and W. C. Borman, eds., *Personnel Selection in Organizations*, San Francisco, Calif.: Jossey-Bass, 1993, pp. 71–98.

Burton, N. W., and L. Ramist, *Predicting Success in College: SAT Studies of Classes Graduating Since 1980*, New York: The College Board, Report No. 2001-2, 2001.

Camara, W. J., and G. Echternacht, *The SAT I and High School Grades: Utility in Predicting Success in College*, New York: The College Board, Office of Research and Development, Research Note RN-10, 2000.

Campion, M. A., D. K. Palmer, and J. E. Campion, "A Review of Structure in the Selection Interview," *Personnel Psychology*, Vol. 50, 1977, pp. 655–702.

Carretta, T. R., *Basic Attributes Test (BAT) System: A Preliminary Evaluation*, Brooks AFB, Tex.: Air Force Human Resources Laboratory, AD-A188-503, November 1987.

———, "Cross Validation of Experimental USAF Pilot Training Performance Models," *Military Psychology*, Vol. 2, No. 4, 1990, pp. 257–264.

———, "Group Differences on US Air Force Pilot Selection Tests," *International Journal of Selection and Assessment*, Vol. 5, No. 2, 1997, pp. 115–127.

———, *Development and Validation of the Test of Basic Aviation Skills (TBAS)*, Wright-Patterson AFB, Ohio: Human Effectiveness Directorate, AFRL-HE-WP-TR-2005-0172, November 2005.

Carretta, T. R., and F. M. Siem, *Personality, Attitudes, and Pilot Training Performance: Final Analysis*, Brooks AFB, Tex.: Air Force Human Resources Laboratory, AFHRL-TP-88-23, October 1988.

Chan, K., F. Drasgow, and L. L. Sawin, "What Is the Shelf Life of a Test? The Effect of Time on the Psychometrics of a Cognitive Ability Test Battery," *Journal of Applied Psychology*, Vol. 84, 1999, pp. 610–619.

Cleary, T. A., "Test Bias: Prediction of Grades of Negro and White Students in Integrated Colleges," *Journal of Educational Measurement*, Vol. 5, No. 2, 1968, pp. 115–124.

Cohen, J., "The Cost of Dichotomization," *Applied Psychological Measurement*, Vol. 7, No. 3, 1983, pp. 249–253.

———, "A Power Primer," *Psychological Bulletin*, Vol. 112, 1992, pp. 155–159.

College Board, "SAT Percentile Ranks: Critical Reading, Mathematics, and Writing," 2009a. As of July 17, 2009:
http://www.collegeboard.com/prod_downloads/highered/ra/sat/SAT_percentile_ranks.pdf

———, "Fact Sheet," 2009b. As of July 17, 2009:
http://www.collegeboard.com/about/news_info/sat/factsheet.html

———, "Final Test Specifications for the New SAT," 2009c. As of July 17, 2009:
http://www.collegeboard.com/prod_downloads/sat/final_test_specifications.pdf

Cowan, D. K., L. E. Barrett, and T. G. Wegner, *Air Force Reserve Officer Training Corps Selection System Validation*, Brooks AFB, Tex.: Air Force Human Resources Laboratory, AFHRL-TR-88-54, December 1989.

Cullen, M. J., C. M. Hardison, and P. R. Sackett, "Using SAT-Grade and Ability-Job Performance Relationships to Test Predictions Derived from Stereotype Threat Theory," *Journal of Applied Psychology*, Vol. 89, 2004, pp. 220–230.

De Corte, W., F. Lievens, and P. R. Sackett, "Combining Predictors to Achieve Optimal Trade-Offs Between Selection Quality and Adverse Impact," *Journal of Applied Psychology*, Vol. 92, 2007, pp. 1380–1393.

Department of the Air Force, *Officer Qualifying Test Information Pamphlet*, AFPT 997, n.d. As of July 17, 2009:
http://www.airforce.com/pdf/AFOQT_S_Pamphlet_REV.pdf

Diehl, G. E., *Correlation Among SAT, ACT, AFOQT and Grade Point Average*, Maxwell AFB, Ala.: Air University, AD-A190-251, January 1986.

Dipboye, R. L., and B. B. Gaugler, "Cognitive and Behavioral Processes in the Selection Interview," in N. Schmitt and W. C. Borman, eds., *Personnel Selection in Organizations*, San Francisco, Calif.: Jossey-Bass, 1993, pp. 135–170.

EASI·Consult, LLC, Kenneth L. Schwartz, and Johnny J. Weissmuller, *Air Force Officer Qualifying Test (AFOQT) Composite Structure Validation: Subgroup Qualification Rates*, Final Report, Deliverable #2, FA3089-07-F-0483 (FMLO-FR-2009-0001), Randolph AFB, Tex.: Force Management Liaison Office, HQ Air Force Personnel Center, 2008.

Equal Employment Opportunity Commission, Civil Service Commission, Department of Labor and Department of Justice, "Uniform Guidelines on Employee Selection Procedures," *Federal Register,* Vol. 43, 1978, pp. 38290–38315.

Finegold, L. S., and D. Rogers, *Relationship Between Air Force Officer Qualifying Test Scores and Success in Air Weapons Controller Training*, Brooks AFB, Tex.: Air Force Systems Command, AD-A158-162, June 1985.

Goldberg, L. R., J. A. Johnson, H. W. Eber, R. Hogan, M. C. Ashton, C. R. Cloninger, and H. C. Gough, "The International Personality Item Pool and the Future of Public-Domain Personality Measures," *Journal of Research in Personality*, No. 40, 2006, pp. 84–96.

Gottfredson, L. S., "Why *g* Matters: The Complexity of Everyday Life," *Intelligence*, Vol. 24, 1997, pp. 79–132.

Hartke, D. D., and Lt Col L. O. Short, USAF, *Validity of the Academic Aptitude Composite of the Air Force Officer Qualifying Test (AFOQT),* Brooks AFB, Tex.: Air Force Systems Command, AD-A194-753, April 1988.

Hough, L. M., and D. S. Ones, "The Structure, Measurement, Validity, and Use of Personality Variables in Industrial, Work, and Organizational Psychology," in N. Anderson, D. S. Ones, H. K. Sinangil, and C. Viswesvaran, eds., *Handbook of Industrial, Work and Organizational Psychology, Volume 1: Personnel Psychology,* Thousand Oaks, Calif.: Sage Publications Ltd, 2002, pp. 233–277.

Hough, L. M., and F. L. Oswald, "Personnel Selection: Looking Toward the Future— Remembering the Past," *Annual Review in Psychology*, Vol. 51, 2000, pp. 631–664.

Hough, L. M., F. L. Oswald, and R. E. Ployhart, "Determinants, Detection and Amelioration of Adverse Impact in Personnel Selection Procedures: Issues, Evidence and Lessons Learned," *International Journal of Selection and Assessment*, Vol. 9, 2001, pp. 152–194.

Huffcutt, A. I., and P. L. Roth, "Racial Group Differences in Employment Interview Evaluations," *Journal of Applied Psychology*, Vol. 83, 1998, pp. 179–189.

Huffcutt, A. I., P. L. Roth, and M. A. McDaniel, "A Meta-Analytic Investigation of Cognitive Ability in Employment Interview Evaluations: Moderating Characteristics and Implications for Incremental Validity," *Journal of Applied Psychology*, Vol. 81, 1996, pp. 459–473.

Hulin, C. L., R. A. Henry, and S. L. Noon, "Adding a Dimension: Time as a Factor in the Generalizability of Predictive Relationships," *Psychological Bulletin*, Vol. 107, 1990, pp. 328–340.

Humphreys, L. G., "Individual Differences," *Annual Reviews in Psychology,* Vol. 3, No. 1, 1952, pp. 131–150.

Hunter, J. E., and R. F. Hunter, "Validity and Utility of Alternative Predictors of Job Performance," *Personnel Bulletin*, Vol. 96, 1984, pp. 72–98.

Ingerick, M., *Identifying Leader Talent: Alternative Predictors for U.S. Air Force Junior Officer Selection and Assessment*, Alexandria, Va.: Human Resources Research Organization, FR-05-47, November 2006. As of November 20, 2008:
http://www.icodap.org/papers/Reports/ALT_PREDICTORS_Report_Nov2006.pdf

Keil, C. T., and J. M. Cortina, "Degradation of Validity over Time: A Test and Extension of Ackerman's Model," *Psychological Bulletin*, Vol. 127, 2001, pp. 673–697.

Kobrin, J. L., B. F. Patterson, E. J. Shaw, K. D. Mattern, and S. M. Barbuti, *Validity of the SAT for Predicting First-Year College Grade Point Average*, New York: The College Board, Report No. 2008-5, 2008.

Kobrin, J. L., V. Sathy, and E. J. Shaw, *A Historical View of Subgroup Performance Differences on the SAT Reasoning Test*, New York: The College Board, Report No. 2006-5, 2007.

Kuncel, N. R., and S. A. Hezlett, "Standardized Tests Predict Graduate Students' Success," *Science,* Vol. 315, February 23, 2007a, pp. 1080–1081.

———, Response to "The Utility of Standardized Tests," *Science,* Vol. 316, June 22, 2007b, pp. 1696–1697.

Kuncel, N. R., S. A. Hezlett, and D. S. Ones, "Academic Performance, Career Potential, Creativity, and Job Performance: Can One Construct Predict Them All?" *Journal of Personality and Social Psychology,* Vol. 86, 2004, pp. 148–161.

Lautenschlager, G. J., and J. L. Mendoza, "A Step-Down Hierarchical Multiple Regression Analysis for Examining Hypotheses About Test Bias in Prediction," *Applied Psychological Measurement,* Vol. 10, No. 2, 1986, p. 133.

Lawrence, I. M., G. W. Rigol, T. Van Essen, and C. A. Jackson, *A Historical Perspective on the Content of the SAT,* New York: The College Board, Report No. 2003-3, ETS RR-03-10, 2003.

Lenning, I. T., *Predictive Validity of the ACT Tests at Selective Colleges,* Iowa City, Ia.: ACT Publications, ERIC No. ED115700, 1975.

Lentz, E., W. C. Bormann, R. H. Bryant, and T. R. Dullaghan, *Air Force Officer Qualifying Test (AFOQT) Trend Analysis,* Tampa, Fla.: Personnel Decisions Research Institutes, Inc., Technical Report No. 618, 2008.

Mael, F. A., "A Conceptual Rationale for the Domain and Attributes of Biodata Items," *Personnel Psychology,* Vol. 44, Winter 1991, pp. 763–791.

Mathews, J. J., *Racial Equity in Selection in Air Force Officer Training School and Undergraduate Flying Training,* Lackland Air Force Base, Tex.: Air Force Human Resources Laboratory, Personnel Research Division, Report No. AFHRL-TR-77-22, 1977.

Mattern, K. D., B. F. Patterson, E. J. Shaw, J. L. Kobrin, and S. M. Barbuti, *Differential Validity and Prediction of the SAT,* New York: The College Board, Report No. 2008-4, 2008.

Maxwell, S. E., and R. D. Arvey, "The Search for Predictors with High Validity and Low Adverse Impact: Compatible or Incompatible Goals?" *Journal of Applied Psychology,* No. 78, 1993, pp. 433–437.

Meyer, G. M., S. E. Finn, L. D. Eyde, G. G. Kay, K. L. Moreland, R. R. Dies, E. J. Eisman, T. W. Kubiszyn, and G. M. Reed, "Psychological Testing and Psychological Assessment, A Review of Evidence and Issues," *American Psychologist,* Vol. 56, No. 2, February 2001, pp. 128–165.

Morgan, R., *Analysis of the Predictive Validity of the SAT and High School Grades from 1976 to 1985,* New York: The College Board, Report No. 89-7, 1989.

Morgeson, F. P., M. A. Campion, R. L. Dipboye, J. R. Hollenbeck, K. Murphy, and N. Schmitt, "Are We Getting Fooled Again? Coming to Terms with Limitations in the Use of Personality Tests for Personnel Selection," *Personnel Psychology,* Vol. 60, No. 3, Autumn 2007, pp. 1029–1049.

Nunnally, J. C., and I. H. Bernstein, eds., *Psychometric Theory,* New York: McGraw-Hill, 1994.

Ones, D. S., and C. Viswesvaran, "Integrity Tests and Other Criterion-Focused Occupational Personality Scales (COPS) Used in Personnel Selection," *International Journal of Selection and Assessment,* Vol. 9, 2001, pp. 31–39.

Ones, D. S., C. Viswesvaran, and F. L. Schmidt, "Comprehensive Meta-Analysis of Integrity Test Validities: Findings and Implications for Personnel Selection and Theories of Job Performance," *Journal of Applied Psychology,* Vol. 78, 1993, pp. 679–703.

Ployhart, R. E., and B. C. Holtz, "The Diversity-Validity Dilemma: Strategies for Reducing Racioethnic and Sex Subgroup Differences and Adverse Impact in Selection," *Personnel Psychology,* Vol. 61, 2008, pp. 153–172.

Public Law 102-166, *The Civil Rights Act of 1991,* November 21, 1991.

Ree, M. J., and T. R. Carretta, *Interchangeability of Verbal and Quantitative Scores for Personnel Selection: An Example,* Brooks AFB, Tex.: Air Force Research Laboratory, Human Effectiveness Directorate, AL/HR-TP-1997-0016, September 1998.

Ree, M. J., T. R. Carretta, and J. A. Earles, "Salvaging Construct Equivalence Through Equating," *Personality and Individual Differences,* Vol. 35, 2003, pp. 1293–1305.

Ree, M. J., T. R. Carretta, and M. S. Teachout, "Role of Ability and Prior Job Knowledge in Complex Training Performance," *Journal of Applied Psychology*, Vol. 80, No. 6, 1995, pp. 721–730.

Robbert, A. A., S. M. Drezner, J. E. Boon, L. M. Hanser, S. C. Moore, L. Scott, and H. J. Shukiar, *Integrated Planning for the Air Force Senior Leader Workforce: Background and Methods*, Santa Monica, Calif.: RAND Corporation, TR-175-AF, 2004. As of August 5, 2009:
http://www.rand.org/pubs/technical_reports/TR175/

Roberts, H. E., and J. Skinner, "Gender and Racial Equity of the Air Force Officer Qualifying Test in Officer Training School Selection Decisions," *Military Psychology,* Vol. 8, No. 2, 1996, pp. 95–113.

Roth, P. L., C. A. Bevier, P. Bobko, F. S. Switzer, and P. Tyler "Ethnic Group Differences in Cognitive Ability in Employment and Educational Settings: A Meta-Analysis," *Personnel Psychology*, Vol. 54, 2001, pp. 297–330.

Sackett, P. R., M. J. Borneman, and B. S. Connelly, "High-Stakes Testing in Higher Education and Employment; Appraising the Evidence for Validity and Fairness," *American Psychologist*, Vol. 63, 2008, pp. 215–227.

Sackett, P. R., and J. E. Ellingson, "The Effects of Forming Multi-Predictor Composites on Group Differences and Adverse Impact," *Personnel Psychology*, Vol. 50, 1997, pp. 707–721.

Sackett, P. R., N. Schmitt, J. E. Ellingson, and M. B. Kabin, "High-Stakes Testing in Employment, Credentialing and Higher Education; Prospects in a Post-Affirmative-Action World," *American Psychologist*, Vol. 56, 2001, pp. 302–318.

Salgado, J. F., C. Viswesvaran, and D. S. Ones, "Predictors Used for Personnel Selection: An Overview of Constructs, Methods and Techniques," in N. Anderson, D. S. Ones, H. K. Sinangil, C. Viswesvaran, eds., *Handbook of Industrial, Work and Organizational Psychology,* Thousand Oaks, Calif.: Sage Publications Ltd., Vol. 1, 2002, pp. 165–199.

Schmidt, F. L., "The Problem of Group Differences in Ability Test Scores in Employment Selection," *Journal of Vocational Behavior*, No. 33, 1988, pp. 272–292.

Schmidt, F. L., and J. E. Hunter, "The Validity and Utility of Selection Methods in Personnel Psychology: Practical and Theoretical Implications of 85 Years of Research Findings," *Psychology Bulletin*, Vol. 124, 1998, pp. 262–274.

Schmitt, J., M. Cortina, M. J. Ingerick, and D. Wiechmann, "Personnel Selection and Employee Performance," in W. C. Borman, D. R. Ilgen, and R. J. Klimoski, eds., *Handbook of Psychology: Volume 12: Industrial and Organizational Psychology*, Hoboken, N.J.: Wiley, 2003, pp. 77–105.

Schmidt, F. L., J. E. Hunter, A. N. Outerbridge, and S. Goff, "The Joint Relation of Experience and Ability with Job Performance: A Test of Three Hypotheses," *Journal of Applied Psychology,* Vol. 73, 1988, pp. 46–57.

Schmidt, F. L., J. E. Hunter, H. C. Taylor, and J. T. Russell, "The Relationship of Validity Coefficients to the Practical Effectiveness of Tests in Selection: Discussion and Tables," *Journal of Applied Psychology*, Vol. 23, 1939, pp. 565–578.

Taylor, H. C., and J. T. Russell, "The Relationship of Validity Coefficients to the Practical Effectiveness of Tests in Selection: Discussion and Tables," *Journal of Applied Psychology*, Vol. 23, 1939, pp. 565–578.

United States Air Force Academy, admissions information. As of July 17, 2009:
http://academyadmissions.com/

United States Air Force ROTC—Qualifying Test, 2009.
As of May 6, 2009:
http://www.afrotc.com/admissions/qualifyingTest.php

Valentine, L. D., Jr., and J. A. Creager, *Officer Selection and Classification Tests: Their Development and Use*, Lackland AFB, Tex.: Aeronautical Systems Division, Air Force Systems Command, AD 269-827, October 1961.

White, L. A., M. C. Young, and M. G. Rumsey, "ABLE Implementation Issues and Related Research," in J. P. Campbell and D. J. Knapp, eds., *Exploring the Limits in Personnel Selection and Classification*. Mahwah, N.J.: Lawrence Erlbaum Associates, 2001.

Wilson, K. M., *A Review of Research on the Prediction of Academic Performance after the Freshman Year*, New York: College Board, Report No. 83-2, 1983.

Young, J., *Differential Validity, Differential Prediction, and College Admission Testing: A Comprehensive Review and Analysis*, New York: College Board, Report No. 2001-62001, 2001.

Zwick, R., *Rethinking the SAT: The Future of Standardized Testing in University Admission*, New York, London: Routledge-Falmer, 2004.